MEMORANDUM IN A CRUET

Memorandum in a Cruet
By
3ichael 7ambert

Dedicated to my people of Colorado

MEMORANDUM IN A CRUET

Intro

Take a Journey through the mind of 3ichael
7ambert.

Table of Contents

MEMORANDUM IN A CRUET

Act I

Introduction

Pangea

In a world like this what am I to believe?
How is this world supposed to be perceived?
A rhythm or two is how I'll talk,
I quite enjoy life's little walk.
In the beginning, all God had to do was snap.
And thus created life's master map.
A galaxy forming in just seven days,
Our God is learning to play.
Mountains Spark forth from the balls of torch.
Seas rise up devouring the beach porch.
Lucifer wasn't perfect and tried to over rule our king.
Banished to the seas, a legend is he.
Deceitful and wicked, without a key.
Lucifer evolved on the everlasting earth,
a serpent was he from birth.
It is not possible to snake charm him.
For he was God's perfect little sin.
The only creature to never stop growing.
A dragon was he, fire blowing.

As time went on, he found some bombs.
The creature that is known to have thumbs.
He snake charmed Eve, and could you believe.
She took from the tree, amnesia'd the free.
With Adam she shared, An apple with care.
As God came down, they ran away.
They had absolutely nothing to say.
They hid ta-tas and a ding dong.
And prepared the worlds first song.

Leaves covered them from head to toe.
God gave them the look that he does know.
He sent them away from the Garden of Eden,
He did not want them to be a beating.
Today, if you go into a museum.
'Lucy' was from the Garden of Eden.
Kids were born who were conscious.
Who began to focus on the science.
Other animals were left at peace,
Or they were to become extinct.
Dodos, Mammoths, and Saber-tooths.
Satan was a Dinosaur who once ruled.

MEMORANDUM IN A CRUET

'Terrible Lizard' in Greek Mythology,
Quite similar to Roman theology.
The term Dinosaur comes from 1842,
From a paleontologist named Owen.
A third of the angels were with Satan,
Ruling the Earth, always out hating.
Mesopotamia is another name for this land,
Where the apple was eaten by a man.
On the outskirts of this great Garden,
The world's first city was being born.
Babylon, our place that was much better.
We had begun to change the weather.
A tower was built to reach to Heaven.
God planned the Earth to end at Eleven.
This island of a Garden and a hot beach,
Was starting to flood as they had preached.
This city of great magnitude and pure power,
It is the time of the city that fell into the water.
Atlantis once called with other names too,
Angels walked the Earth, quite a few.

Aries, an Angel from Mars, was in charge of the
Great War.
Aphrodite's and Cupid, spread Love and more.
Empires to be build as time went on,
The Jews were assigned to pass it on.
Let's start a new, without Satan making Earth hell,
It's too late, for the tree made us unwell.
Good thing a conscious comes with this sin,
For pure evil will never have the chance to win.
The world was different, an ozone layer held water.
This water was to start the fire,
Prophets began to Journal-a-jotter.
An asteroid collision disrupted the silver wire.
Forty days of rain came from above,
The remains of the asteroid's love.
Is what we call the moon today,
It is hung out on all our days.

MEMORANDUM IN A CRUET

As the tides of a Great Flood began to surrender,
The Earth again was fresh and tender.
People spread worldwide as continents began to form,
To counter act this unity, racism was born.
Yellow, White, Black, and Brown.
All flaunting knowledge like a clown.
To kill each other and ourselves.
We ate from the tree, we are not well.
The Mayans and Aztecs will tell you it's in the stars.
Zodiac beliefs will advance you far.
Pharaohs and Persians were the original Punk Rock.
They took control and wore fancy socks.
Pyramids and Walls, Towers and Roads.
Society, I don't think that we should gloat.
We claim to be better, while claiming to be nothing.
This attitude should change, it's really sucking.

Until the day, that Jesus walked the Earth,
Spirits were allowed to have rebirths.
Fallen angels would create 'Demi God's with us.
How is consciousness, a sin to lust?
We're the only ones that are able to love,
It's a Gift of Punishment from up above.
Love and Hate, Greed and Feud.
Without that tree, we'd have no mood.

Let's fix a place that was once perfect,
Let's survive in what we call the market.
Let's mix chemicals to better ourselves.
Let's mix chemicals to kill ourselves.
Let us be smart and arrogant to all.
Let us die when our empire falls.
Let us have what we want.
Let me die for what I want.

MEMORANDUM IN A CRUET

The Jews were mocked from the beginning of time.
Their prophecy tasted like a lime.
Empires over ruled their beliefs.
For they were the Master Chief.
It seems though this is all connected,
Through everything now is infected.
Many Jews will not accept their Prophet.
And we're still waiting for Muhammad.
Jehovah or Allah, what is your name?
Tell me and I shall bring you fame.

These Prophecies have existed since the beginning of time,
All we have to do is read between the lines.
For in the Bible, Hades exists. Other translations have more to list.
The Greek Empire was the first to plumb,
Again, let's thank God for these thumbs.
The Greeks turned Angels into Gods,
The Romans, turned Planets into Gods.
Partly Sci-Fi, Partly Magical.
The time had come for the kingdom to fall.

Ahead of their time and doing quite well,
Dark ages came let's experience hell.
The renaissance was to rebuild the great,
In a sense we opened a different gate.

We took the path to obtain great knowledge,
In a world to succeed you must be in college.
Electricity and Fossil Fuels,
Earth's Treasure, these Rule.

Industrial Age has come to pass,
This digital era is meant to last.

The end might come soon for all we know,
We think we have forever to live though.

MEMORANDUM IN A CRUET

Some went off to become pirates,
Rape and Pillage was their fair bet.
To live a full life from our King,
Drinking Rum is what they'd sing.
Nautical Gods like Odin and Thor,
They had Angel DNA in their Core.
Shiva comes from the great East,
The Dahlia Llama might be the messiah we preach.
Everything that happens on Planet Earth,
Like the bomb on Hiroshima, Or your first son's birth.
There is meaning and purpose to it all.
God's Novel of Life, is the best book of them all.
For the black plague and the death of Alexander,
This world without time is grander.
Yellowstone to explode at any given time.
Mayans point that 2012 is in align.
Jews, Chinese, Egyptians will say it's almost time.
Just watch closely for the signs.
We've become to know of a great blind.
It's majestic though, truly one of a kind.

If you take the chance to just open your mind,
You'll learn to live for the very first time.
A comet to say hello in 2029,
But on that day it's just a sign.
To prepare for it in 2036.
Will technology have it's wits.
Nuclear Arms could wipe us all out,
Maybe even before this track is out.
Jerusalem is to be given the people,
The time will come when it's the holy people.
The mark of the beast will rise forth,
During the maximum evil restore.

MEMORANDUM IN A CRUET

I flip this phone around,
What have I found?
An apple that has a bite taken out,
Is this what everyone was talking about?
It's the sign of great knowledge,
This iPhone has an app for college.
The mark of the beast was to be in the hand,
And give you access to all of the land.
Google, in my pocket, well, I know it all.
Seems as if this new empire couldn't fall.
Facebook, we are almost now telepathic,
You give us the ability to be omni-presentamatic.
To decipher writings that come from beyond,
It'll take an eternity in a peaceful pond.

The Eastern world appears to be under a separate covenant,
Or for a time once was different.
If the Chinese gathered up in arms,
Every American would be alarmed.
Ages 0 - Death, fighting plenty,
Everyone would have to kill twenty.
Possibilities exist and around a corner they lure.
This world still has many years to mature.
For The Messiah is to return to Planet Earth,
Muslims, Jews, and Christians will be rebirth-ed.
For the day that all will cheer his name,
God is the only one who deserves fame.
The time of Judgement will come before us,
On the day, the meaning of life will become clear to us.

MEMORANDUM IN A CRUET

Act II

Memorandum

2036

Fireworks in the Twilight Sky.
Shooting Stars Pass us by.
Flakes of Snow, Dust the Air.
One last chance to show I care.

Intergalactic sounds break the speed of light.
I'm glad to be given such a stellar sight.
Honoring the Skyline with such intense Light.
Blinding the Mountains, Here we take flight.

Terrorizing screams and bloodshed tears.
A whirlwind of pain surrounding our fears.

Leaves of Snow.
Dirts of Wind.
Physical form within
Our Sin.

For a moment, For a feeling.
A song will convey meaning.

Dim the lights, Hear the Sounds.
Can you Feel, What's all around?
Rushing winds, Roaring Sounds.
Hairs stand up, as we leave the ground.

Beneath our feet, we stand alone.
Above the stars, lives our home.

September Sounds (Lose Your Mind)

What does it feel like to lose your mind, to truly be just one of our kind.
To feel outcast in a vast lonely world, while being in a harsh little world.
What does it feel like to have Energy, what does it feel like to be just like me?
To do the unspeakable on such harsh terms, To grow your mind as we all learn.

What is it about you that they say is so wrong,
Why have they been doing this to you for so long?
It is okay, for you are not alone!
We're taking this long ride home.

Why did she do this to you and why does it hurt?
Why must you push yourself to limit alert?
Why is it that you defend with a spill?
When may you be going in for the kill?
Where is this world where you've once reigned?
Why is it that you claim no shame?
When does Big Ben strike high noon?
Why is it that they call you a loon?
Who is the one that told you you're no good?
Why is it they kicked you down to the hood?
How do you dare to claim amounts of pity.
Channel that Strength into Eternal Witty.

The One Thing; I Don't Deserve

There is only one thing I yearn
for and it is a simple girl,
The one to cuddle with to
movies and show to the world.
There is one thing I yearn for,
and she has to be a friend,
Someone that has patience to
build a bond into the end.

The One Thing I yearn for, I do
not Deserve,
The Relationship to Relax while
in the Curve.
The One Thing I yearn for, I
always push away,
I am afraid someone will get
hurt on this day.

The One Thing I yearn for is to
be in arms in a night like this,
Instead of meeting
acquaintances with you, the
sea of fish.
The One Thing I yearn for is to
take you out at a nice place,
Instead of all this Art, and
attempting to win the Sacred
race.

The One Thing I yearn for, I do
not Deserve,
The Relationship to Relax while
in the Curve.
The One Thing I yearn for, I
always push away,
I am afraid someone will get
hurt on this day.

It is ironic to be backed into a
corner,
To be pushed in a solitude for a
loner.
It's a contradiction to be put
right here,
Though it's the place that lost
that fear.
It is ironic that I do not deserve
to Love,
To be pushed in a corner to
shout above.
It's a contradiction to be the
One as me,
Maybe I'll find my happiness,
to be free.

The One Thing I yearn for, I do
not Deserve,
The Relationship to Relax while
in the Curve.
The One Thing I yearn for, I
always push away,
I am afraid someone will get
hurt on this day.
The One Thing I yearn for, I do
not Deserve,
The Relationship to Relax while
in the Curve.
The One Thing I yearn for, I
always push away,
I am afraid someone will get
hurt on this day.

Left Behind (To Lead)

A duo of relationships spending an afternoon in the summer sun,
A pair of best friends walking the city streets for that vacation fun.
Swimming in the streams for recreation in the native parts of our land,
A teenage dream beats the heart for the family as loud as he can.

In her yard, the birds flew past,
To witness one who fell in last.
He was left behind to be a lead, To conquer the serenity of greed.
Three teenagers helped That One dying for the Life to be Free,
From the Chamber pulling apart his trust, which blinded the sea.
One sibling through a chair as they began to play and build a bond,
Which led to the Pen on Paper of a Dream as he finally had to yawn.

In her yard, the birds flew past,
To witness one who fell in last.
He was left behind to be a lead, To conquer the serenity of greed.

His best friend once showed him what it is like to truly have trust and love,
If he was a 'chick', he would make sure he would be his special little dove.
This Group led to the One he had sworn was his Dear Angel from above,
Though the wings glided him through new broken friends, and to Love.

In her yard, the birds flew past,
To witness one who fell in last.
He was left behind to be a lead, To conquer the serenity of greed.
In her yard, the birds flew past,
To witness one who fell in last.
He was left behind to be a lead, To conquer the serenity of greed.

MEMORANDUM IN A CRUET

I'll Never Unlove You (The Hopeless Romantic)

It was in the Commons of Rangeview High,
Where your Beauty enchanted a song into my eyes.
In that moment, everything seemed to wash away,
Into Cupid's Arrow which broke my knee that Day.
A Year of having you as my closest dear friend,
It was the Year of my Deadly departed end.
In the time of crisis I fled to you for guidance,
Through that moment I gained my Audience.

You broke my Heart, by my own Fault.
So then I diluted my feelings into a Vault.
To then beckon my Dreams by Default.
To Face you again, and put it all on Halt.

Then again I made more mistakes then we could count,
There's one thing for sure my Love will never un-mount.
When my Heart broke I shared my love with everyone,
But now as it lays broken twice, I refuse to love One.
I'll Love our Homeland and everyone residing,
Inside these huts on these hills, as they are confiding.
I'm sorry, sincerely, if my Art depresses you at all,
But I'm doing this for me, and with you I expect no call.

You broke my Heart, by my own Fault.
So then I diluted my feelings into a Vault.
To then beckon my Dreams by Default.
To Face you again, and put it all on Halt.

I poked your heart with a needle, as you threw mine far away,
To then have your new Horse trample on your's one day.
Then I rushed to take your heart back at the solemn chance,
In front of everyone there, which disrupted the cosmic balance.
Then the it turned and we both went into my deep dark hell,
I heard you are doing okay and that you're doing quite well.
That kiss we shared, and holding your hand, brought me back,
Into the place where my life does not seem so dark and whack.

You broke my Heart, by my own Fault.
So then I diluted my feelings into a Vault.
To then beckon my Dreams by Default.
To Face you again, and put it all on Halt.

Though they stared, and we both landed in the gutter,
I want you to know it's when I began to gaze and stutter.
It's when my stress let loose and I became self-conscious,
I'm sorry I couldn't trust you, but I owed you my concept.
Of if I dare named you, then they all must be named.
Which began fire to my label of 'The Drama Queen Game'.
Then the one you left me for, had to have been called out,
Now I'm Free, and that's what this Novel is apparently about.

MEMORANDUM IN A CRUET

Jesus was a Carpenter

I tied her avidly, upon the train tracks,
Then watched the locomotive bypass,
The Hearts Chained to choke in a Chamber,
With Chromatic Steal shifting Embers.
Reflecting the Image of unusual colors,
Glowing upon the Dew of the Flower.
It was Love that destroyed the world,
Over the Letter to God, About the One Girl.
As a Dramatic Poet Seeking it's Refuge,
The World Ended Gracefully in a Solitude.
Where the Spiritual Journey came it's course,
A Stampede tore Apart A Pale White Horse.
Which led to the Flames abiding in the Clouds,
For Exodus 7:11 says there's One here Now.
"Pharaoh then summoned wise men and sorcerers,
and the Egyptian magicians also did the same things by their secret arts:"
Art of Life, to reunite and to then Fall Apart,
Celibate Life for the Love of my Dear Art.
The Royal began with breathing a Fire,
Slaying the Dragon attached on the Wire,
Evolving the Puppet into a Soulful Robot,
Fusing minds with the Dinosaurs we got,
Welding the steel in the flames on a Knight,
That could summon an Asteroid of Light,
To Exile the Vultures, Preying on the Land.
Revelation 13:13 Explains of a No-Mad-Man.
"And he performed great and miraculous signs,
even causing fire to come down from heaven to earth in full view of men. "

A Blasphemous Lie over the Death of itself,
For the Living Lord on a Sacrificial Shelf,
To Intimidate the lesser side of The Love,
To Reign a Fire to Unite the Damage Above.
Caused from the Situation of a Lost Arc,
Encasing the stray animals in the Park,
To tame and release inside a Dead Demon,
Revelation 11:5 Is the Preaching of Semen.
"If anyone tries to harm them, fire comes from their mouths and devours their enemies.
This is how anyone who wants to harm them must die."
The Family of the Carpenter opened the lids,
To Crumble the Cookies he had once hid,
With his Pennies concealed in a piggy bank,
Tied upon a mast of the Wooden Old Plank.
Sacrificing Omens on the Cross of the Cloth,
With the Flag waving the Betrayed Dull Moth,
In the midst of the Crew waiting on the Deck,
With Luke 9:54 depicting my name as Heck.
"When the disciples James and John saw this, they asked,
'Lord, do you want us to call fire down from heaven to destroy them?'"

MEMORANDUM IN A CRUET

Which is the Moment for God unlike the 'Best',
To Gather the Sins we have and Lay them to Rest,
Which Reveals Saul as the Phoenix of Old Paul,
To Martyr the Soul, in Front of them all,
To Release the Karma and Send the Balance,
In the Hopes to Save Man Kind by a Chance,
Off to Oppose the Bad Luck of the Mirror,
To Butterfly the Effect of Passionate Deceiver,
Through the Lands to Revolutionize our mind,
1 Kings 18:38 Outreaches to Her own Kind.
"Then the fire of the LORD fell and burned up the sacrifice, the wood,
the stones and the soil, and also licked up the water in the trench."

Jesus I do this for you in my House of Love,
Will you find my message in a bottle Above?
With Hands Held High For You To Lift Me Up,
And to Let me Taste the wine of your Holy Cup,
You're the King Reigning the Progressive Altar,
I bow to you as The Prince Straight Out of Hell,Psalm 28:2
For the Reason to Repent Farewell."Hear my cry for mercy as I call to you for help,
as I lift up my hands toward your Most Holy Place."

The Prince of Darkness Dictates the social army,
To rise above the fighting in the Aero-Military,
To Unite Humanity In the Name of Our Love,1 Timothy 2:8
Describes the Peace I Yearn Above,
"I want men everywhere to lift up holy hands in prayer, without anger or disputing. "

I Plea to Not Burn in Hell, But to Set everything Well
To Pray for Peace From You, Exodus 8:4 Sacrificing You
"Sacrifice the other lamb at twilight with the same grain offering and
its drink offering as in the morning--a pleasing aroma,
an offering made to the LORD by fire."
The Devil Wears Prada in a Sick Pride,
The Yin and a Yang twirling the Stride,
It's Human Nature To Sin in a Parallel,
1 Kings 22:21 Is the Reason I Fell.Below.
"Finally, a spirit came forward, stood before the LORD and said, 'I will entice him.'"
As The Gemini of the Demon of Light,
Becoming the magnitude of the fight,
Here to Sacrifice the Other Lamb on Sight,
Matthew 24:40 Lord taketh the might.
"Two men will be out in the field; one will be taken, and one will be left."

I'm A Living Sacrifice With the Dear Confession,
We are not Meant to talk with this Congestion,
In a world of Humans fighting others far away,
1 Corinthians 15:51-52 Is what I am here to Say.
"we will all be changed, in an instant, in the blink of an eye, at the last trumpet"

MEMORANDUM IN A CRUET

The Trumpet of the Loudest Melody in the Heavens,
Sending Prayers and Wishes upon eleven eleven,
With the message up upon the carrier Pigeon,
Revelation 11:11 Speaks of the half of the Seven.
"And after three days and an half the Spirit of life
from God entered into them, and they stood upon their feet; and great fear fell upon them which saw them."

The Companions in the Sea of Clouds,
Unite as One as the God of the Crowd,
Majestically Releasing the Evil of humanity,
1 Thessalonians 4 :17 bestows our sanity.
"Then we who are alive, who are left,
will be caught up together with them in the clouds to meet the Lord in the air.
Thus we shall always be with the Lord."

Translating the Bible into our Armageddon,
Seems to be the End of what we once mentioned,
Am I the Anti-Christ During this World War,
Revelation 6:17 Because of a Mind gone Far?
"For the great day of their wrath has come, and who can stand?"

Migraine

Everlasting fountains bleeding hope for chivalry.
Devastation erupts new direction with society.
Cancer consumes wills and the faint of heart.
Prayers glisten amongst the stars, please don't part.

Migraines spark forth competing the wins.
The battlefield transforms to chaos again.
Once upon a time our ways were just,
Learn to think is a must.

Clouds strike psychotic paper-cuts into our brains.
Shove it and listen, because this is my pain.
Skip through these hollows, you'll see what I mean.
Paralleling the force of Dragonite's magnificent Solar Beam.
Pain loves narcissism in ignorant jokers.
Developing a king that enjoys strip poker.
Ruling over the redundant obstacles that face,
New suns rise with a surprise, now I'm setting the pace.
Symphonic phrases that express my desire and taste.
My potential devours the demons that waste.

When the time is right.
When the time its near.
When the time is mine.
No one shall fear.

The time is tonight.
The time is here.
The time is mine.
May I hear you cheer?

The Gemini Dream (2012)

The twinkle in their fair eyes outmatch that of the stars,
In which the souls mimic the moon's glow spotlighting Mars.
Rays from David's Star detain asteroids, as well as Ex-Pluto.
Fortifying the Sun, from distinct constellations, Viva La Mojo.
The Galactic Alignment is key in the Salvation of Mankind,
One Christmas left until the folklore, 'Twenty Twelve Shine'.
Bodies fiddle with capitalistic rituals as Souls abide in clouds,
Exchanging Enlightenment within the Sea of Fish, Be Loud,
The Corruption of Power scribbles upon a Pagan Stone,
The Illuminati plots Deceit but I'm here to have it be known.
Obsess over the Politics to save our Families dear lives,
We are humans whom mistakenly hate the love strive.

The Gemini Dreams to logically create beauty upon the scene,
Devouring the Conspiracy as a returned favor, as a hate fiend,
Rooted with the Extremities of Love that posses any being,
Freeing His Family into the Enlightenment of For seeing,
The Warfare inside the mind of a strange Youthful nobody,
Where It's Jesus and Lucifer against practically everybody,
Entailing a Memorandum in a Cruet for the Hopes to Die,
To aloft itself into the Vision imprisoning the ability to Fly.

Babylon deteriorated as we reached the Glorious Heavens,
Revealing the Angels that account the Power in Seven,
Mother Earth has the tendency to Cycle the Truth in our Time,
As well as for Lost Atlantis we are Witnessing a Comet Shine,
Across the Blue Sphere twirling crooked through the Galaxy,
For any imperial belief of a Reason to Live in a Fallacy,
The World Is Flat and There exists Not even one True God,
The Fear of the Golden Age sickens Minds from their iPod,
The New World Order may be the most Blissful experience,
If the Rockefellars corrupt our Government, Hop the Fence.
To Mexico or Canada avoiding Amendment of Marshall Law,
The Manuscripts of the Dawn of Time, warned that foresaw.

The Gemini Dreams to logically create beauty upon the scene,
Devouring the Conspiracy as a returned favor, as a hate fiend,
Rooted with the Extremities of Love that posses any being,
Freeing His Family into the Enlightenment of For seeing,
The Warfare inside the mind of a strange Youthful nobody,
Where It's Jesus and Lucifer against practically everybody,
Entailing a Memorandum in a Cruet for the Hopes to Die,
To aloft itself into the Vision imprisoning the ability to Fly.
Up in Arms, it's the Moment to Love, Spread the Message Up High Above,
The Revolution has been Calling, While they happily mock the Falling,
It's Christmas Time, Guide your Family, Into the Better side of Gifted Insanity,
It's the Only way to Protest the Rich, An Armada of Mages to save a Glitch.

Suffocation

Grinding my pain just beneath the lips
Suffocating from rain in this movie clip.
Losing myself when the sun lies to rest.
Evolving my mind and my ways into the best.
Channeling the memories of being consumed by life.
Into the strength to crawl out of the strife.
Away from the dark place titled as life.
Into the dream of being in the arms of my wife.

Suffocation.
Exhibition.
Contemplation.
Motivation.

Like I was strangled by the harsh weather.
This hurricane of drama known as Heather.
When the violent winds crash into my heart,
I develope a taste for shopping at walmart.
A ghetto lifestyle I'm proud not to lie to you.
Ten bucks is all I had once spent on shoes.
EBT cards to let us endure just another day.
Though it also helps us find our way.

Suffocation.
Resignation.
Automation.
Motivation.

The fog comes quick, irritating the pain.
I completely forgot, what is your name?
The love for you has lost a hate reign.
A message in a bottle, it's all the same.
Asking for your company during the typhoon.
So I may lift you to live upon our moon.
Patience is a virtue, please let it be soon.
To take flight after hatching from our cacoon.

Suffocation.
Dedication.
Desiccation.
Motivation.

Suffocation.
Dictation.
Vacation.
Motivation.

Ex-Nextdoor

Now here in my car, I lay alone.
Frowning upon my telephone.
Heart ache over my lost friends,
I'll miss you until the very end.

Here is my one last plea for you,
I miss every single one of you.
The cold shoulder you gave me,
Spawned a dark lonesome insanity.

I just wish you could understand,
That poverty and drugs can kill a man.
I've seen it all from being stolen from,
As my enemies lied to me for the fun.

Starving for days upon days,
Money is apparently the way.
My only wish is to hear your voice.
Hating me was all of your choice.

I know that I've rained texts for days,
Whining and crying over their ways.
I cursed you out when I needed to eat,
And because my life is spent on the street.

You just don't understand from where I come from,
I beg and plea, to be your friend, all you do is shun.
I'm looking for companions to get my mind off this.
To watch a movie, have some fun, and talk is my wish.

I've been chasing this fame for many a year,
Many people know of me didn't you hear?
The fact though, that you're just next door,
Hit me deep, crying down into the core.

It broke me down, and tore me apart.
Reminded me of the pain in my heart.
I avoid everyone that you may know,
Just because I put on this epic show.

Now lets think about this, why am I scared?
Since when did it become wrong to care?
This makes no sense, we all must get along.
I've been through much, I'm quite strong.

I can lead a path to the brighter tomorrow,
This heartless city lets me bleed my sorrow.
If only I was allowed to say hi during lunch,
I'd be able to impress your entire bunch.

Though the fact you would like nothing of me,
I have no choice but to respect that of thee.
It's killing me every single one of these days,
As I pass your people, journeying on my way.

All I truly want is a taste of that Peace,
So I dream we talk again, signing a lease.
I can never forget anything you've told me.
Now here I go yet again, just let me be.

I choose to be the brightest star,
In hopes that it will take me far.
Away from the ghetto-sh life,
Addicts, Theives, Lives, Strife.

There is nothing left of my life from what I can see,
It's a secret I'm leaving, because none will miss me.
I'll fake my death, to make a thousand ones cry,
Ya'll abandoned me, I'm truly not that kind of guy.

MEMORANDUM IN A CRUET

In this moment, death to you all,
As I scream and shout into this fall.
I'm an Artist, it's all about the story.
To make a million, and meet Glory.

My hand is here for you to take,
As for everyone else I'll be fake.
Insiders know exactly who I am,
A guy laughing as much as he can.

I'm worried though that we'll soon cross paths,
You know all about my demons and their wrath.
What is it though that had destroyed my life,
I lost my happiness and hopes of any wife.

You know me well, it is very true,
I never thought I'd abandon you.
I'm different in a few certain ways,
I really thought I'd make your day.

Now alone I write away my thoughts,
Thankful that I am incredibly hot.
I go back and forth from being a trophy,
It's stressful, and as lonely as I can be.

You're amazing girl, and it makes me feel weak,
Knowing you're close hating me every week.
Is a cigarette break with you, too much to ask?
I just want to forget about my own past.

You were there during the darkest of times,
Back when though I could call you all mine.
My deadly world laid waste into your soul,
Misery upon misery, hearts into blackholes.

I owe you the world, and this is my pact,
I'll give it all to you, in due time, in fact.
As I scream out, and get into their heads.
I'm well aware, that this is me, to be dead.

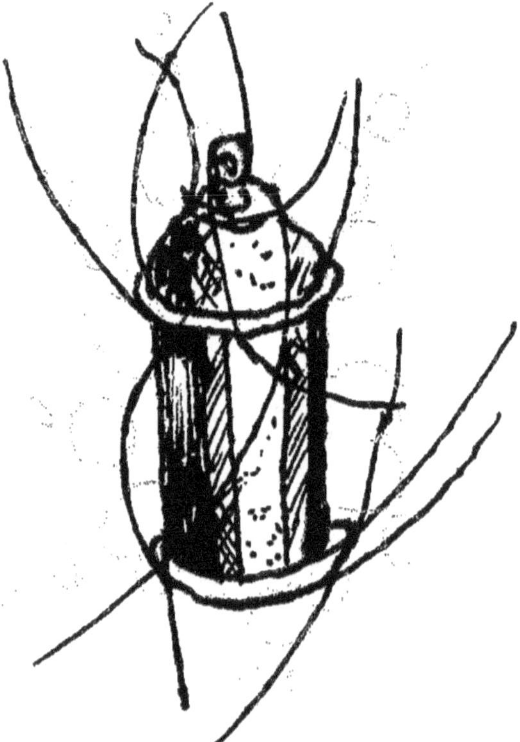

White Ghost (11:11)

Lacking the Significant Other, I build my Ecstatic Empire.
I give birth to the Rolling Riot, Breeding the Omega Fire.
Consuming the attention across the world wide sea.
In many ways in prayers and hopes to set me free.
Through it all, White Ghosts haunt my faded soul.
In the memory of her fair love which birthed this hole.
Black and Deep, infinite space, losing the lustful taste.
Craving divine love, embraced her shove, now I'm above.

Nomads chasing the painted clouds,
Drawing abundant cowardly crowds.
Drifting through hypnotic wormholes,
Phasing gamma rays through souls.

Game Over, My princess lays rest in another castle.
Lusting True Love is my ultimate mission to so tackle.
Without it, it seems, a pointless journey, know what I mean?
To give up, everything I have, including my retrofired lab.
Abandonment here is keyword, evolving me into a bird.
Though I have a 1up life, I my last Mario through strife.
Designing combos and passwords, into the locked world.

Nomads chasing the painted clouds,
Drawing abundant cowardly crowds.
Drifting through hypnotic wormholes,
Phasing gamma rays through souls.

It's my wish for the feeling of Love that I once had,
Gauging eyes out with drama because I'm so 'bad'.
I call it art because I do it eternally so very well.
When I raise the bar, my storms bring all hell.
So what time is it, for you, in your current scene.
Do you have the will and power to plant the bean?
To let the stock grow into the unknown Heaven.
I do this, while wishing, on every eleven:eleven.

MEMORANDUM IN A CRUET

My Midnight Love

'Hi' in the hallway is the moment this fairy tale had begun.
The acquaintance of Love with it's sweet kiss of Death.
I've literally walked one thousand miles since that fun.
Through the tsunamis as devastating as puffed meth.

My midnight love, Our Times were elegant.
Through the Love, our moment's magnificent.
My midnight love, I yearn to gaze into your eyes.
Through the Hate, I'm excelling my life to once fly.

I was the first to teach you how to drive,
You taught me how to feel so alive.
In the darkness you were my savior,
Cataclysm evil abrupt-ed my behavior.
You once told me the sweetest words,
The smile of yours completed my world.
Through the lunches that we once shared,
You laughed at bambi because you cared.

My midnight love, cuddling to the movie.
Through the Love, please believe me.
My midnight love, walking after dark.
Through the hate, yelling by the park.

From the moment you said 'i finally found the right guy'
I've loved you since then without even one white lie.
Years later the pain sinks into my blood flowing deep.
I wander at times wondering where my heart to keep.
I've seen many who would kill to be my darling princess,
The truth though, is without you, I'm the complete mess.

My midnight love, cuddling to the movie.
Through the Love, please believe me.
My midnight love, walking after dark.
Through the hate, yelling by the park.

Those who tell me it's so wrong to Love.
Please learn to care, or Go Kill Yourself.
These feelings of mine are made of Love.
They won't leave, but I'll Happy Myself.
Those who tell me it's so wrong to Love.
Please learn to care, or Go Kill Yourself.
These feelings of mine are made of Love.
They won't leave, but I'll Happy Myself.

Though you left me here with out a trace,
Heading into the future at a steady pace.
My life is becoming everything that I need,
Everything that I want, and to let me feed.
Dreams and Money arriving just as planned.
Becoming a better man, as fast as I can.
Doing it for you, because love is enough,
To be happy when the skies blow rough.

To talk to you, just one more time.
Making the world, the place of mine.
To talk to you, I'll swallow my pride.
Having the world, go off to hide.
To talk to you, just one more time.
Making the world, the place of mine.

MEMORANDUM IN A CRUET

To talk to you, I'll swallow my pride.
Having the world, go off to hide.
To talk to you, just one more time.
Making the world, the place of mine.
To talk to you, I'll swallow my pride.
Having the world, go off to hide.
To talk to you, just one more time.
Making the world, the place of mine.
To talk to you, I'll swallow my pride.
Having the world, go off to hide.

Now Just As Memory To Be My Glue,
Reminiscing The Massages I Gave You
My Favorite Gesture, Displaying My Heart
You Study Massage Therapy As We Part
I Cannot Help But Feel, I Impacted You
Through The Three, That Have Hurt You.
I Was Wrong To Let It All Get To This.
My Wish For You Is To Become The Best.
The Clock Strikes Midnight During The Pain.
I Miss Spending Time With You In The Rain.

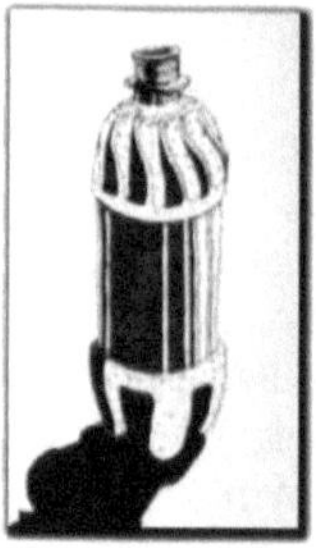

Lucidation

Stimulating my internal membrane elicits modish elation,
Agnate to the transmutation of apprentice into magician.
Abdicating materiality into the terrine of various clout.
Potentiality inexhaustible for aspirations breathe doubt.
Ulterior twilight conjured delinquent aversions,
Interpolated Meditation and Lucidation.
Ulterior twilight manifested sincere dispositions,
Interpolated Meditation and Lucidation.

Squandering acumen by dint of revered anamnesis,
Fusing inclination amidst truth for photosynthesis.
Spawning dimensions along desires to procreate,
With intuition as epoch, abiding in cells for fate.
Utmost twilight conjured delinquent aversions,
Interpolated Meditation and Lucidation.
Utmost twilight manifested sincere dispositions,
Interpolated Meditation and Lucidation.

Concluding tonight, I cottoned to the afterimage of you,
From the realm of divination, to fritter epoch for you.
Lucidating invocations in the solitary habitat with you.
To ajar my optics, distinguishing that there is no you.

Ulterior twilight conjured delinquent aversions,
Interpolated Meditation and Lucidation.
Ulterior twilight manifested sincere dispositions,
Interpolated Meditation and Lucidation.
Utmost twilight conjured delinquent aversions,
Interpolated Meditation and Lucidation.
Utmost twilight manifested sincere dispositions,
Interpolated Meditation and Lucidation.

LEARN

OUTLAST TO

VIRTUES THE

EVOLVE AND

Rave at the Bank

Another new day emerging more pain,
I'm beginning to ponder why I even came.
It's happening, is the reason still the same?
Or have you become a face with a lifeless name?

Into the dream, I dive my head.
Forgetting to relax inside my bed.
Into the bank, to feed my greed.
Dancing with Rage, please take heed.

Escape from the Horror and The Game,
Dancing with Love, Leaving the Pain.
Insanity Breached, Dodging the Ball.
Living with Family, Unite with 'em all.
Escaping the Temptations, That corrupt Lifestyles,
While breathing in the Ravers gone Wild.
Moshing as a Punk consumed with rage,
Family as One, a humane home for this age.

Rave at the bank, let the money Reign,
So many ravers, whom are all the same.
Rave at the bank, let the money Reign.
So many Ravers, in PLUR have came.
Rave at the bank, let the money Reign,
So many ravers, whom are all the same.
Rave at the bank, let the money Reign.
So many Ravers, in PLUR have came.

Another day emerging, wading in the sorrow.
Soul eradicating ones whom become hollow.
Reputations strobe through the city streets,
Into the crossroads that Respect-ions meet.
Peace in the Skyline to breed Love for the Family.
During the warfare loathing pure just insanity.
Emotional vacations intercept honest words,
To talk as Hitler, to Change the World.

For all to get along, all as one.
Is our dream for you, in the sun.
For all to get along, all as one.
Is our dream for you, in the sun.
For all to get along, all as one.
Is our dream for you, in the sun.
For all to get along, all as one.
Is our dream for you, in the sun.

Into the dream, I dive my head.
Forgetting to relax inside my bed.
Into the bank, to feed my greed.
Dancing with Rage, please take heed.

Escape from the Horror and The Game,
Dancing with Love, Leaving the Pain.
Insanity Breached, Dodging the Ball.
Living with Family, Unite with 'em all.
Escaping the Temptations, That corrupt Lifestyles,
While breathing in the Ravers gone Wild.
Moshing as a Punk consumed with rage,
Family as One, a humane home for this age.

Rave at the bank, let the Peace Reign,
So many ravers, whom are all the same.
Rave at the bank, let the Love Reign.
So many Ravers, in PLUR have came.
Rave at the bank, let the Unity Reign,
So many ravers, whom are all the same.
Rave at the bank, let the Respect Reign.
So many Ravers, in PLUR have came.

MEMORANDUM IN A CRUET

I'm a slave of the system.
A slave to the wrath
I'm a slave to you.
And a slave to cash.
I'm a slave to my needs,
A slave in the Lead.
I'm a slave to my sins.
A slave to what's within.

Into the dream, I dive my head.
Forgetting to relax inside my bed.
Into the bank, to feed my greed.
Dancing with Rage, please take heed.
Into the dream, I dive my head.
Forgetting to relax inside my bed.
Into the bank, to feed my greed.
Dancing with Rage, please take heed.

Avenging my Heart by all Means.
Forever Gone, oh so it seems.
To Never Love just One again,
Learned my lesson way back when.
Abundant Love craving Home to rest,
This time for everyone, it's for the best.
To avoid anymore Tragic damage.
To handle my love, by self manage.

NOW
WHAT!?!

Hero and Survivor

A tingle of faint whispers crash landing prophecies into your kingdom,
Imagine the Mayans, being condemned for black magic as the symptom.
Crusades manifesting a black and white scene on the reel of life's Philosophy.
Witnessing heartless Vikings pillaging innocent and corrupt diplomacy.

The Circle of Life, and Loop of Time.
Parasitic Plagues Petrifying Spines.
Lives in Full Circle, Time in a Spiral.
Passionate Doctrines Living Viral.

You feel lost in an alley with no where to go,
Though you survived to have them all know.
That through the dark and the light, a heart of a hero,
Defends family on sight, where temperature's below zero.
A mighty rush of life becomes the hero,
And as the darkness becomes light,
The souls abode webs in the astro,
To never surrender during the Epic Fight.

Goosebumps map out your thoughts crawling up your skin to the history,
Of what once were screams bestowing distress immured in your anatomy.
Legends of the Zodiac preaching a curriculum evading Alcatraz and Psychopaths.
The manuscripts in the Suns breathe that you're okay exploring your chosen path.

The Circle of Life, and Loop of Time.
Parasitic Plagues Petrifying Spines.
Lives in Full Circle, Time in a Spiral.
Passionate Doctrines Living Viral.

You feel lost in an alley with no where to go,
Though you survived to have them all know.
That through the dark and the light, A heart of a hero,
Defends family on sight, Where temperature's below zero.
A mighty rush of life becomes the hero,
And as the darkness becomes light,
The souls abode webs in the astro,
To never surrender during the Epic Fight.

The Circle of Life, and Loop of Time.
Parasitic Plagues Petrifying Spines.
Lives in Full Circle, Time in a Spiral.
Passionate Doctrines Living Viral.
The Circle of Life, and Loop of Time.
Parasitic Plagues Petrifying Spines.
Lives in Full Circle, Time in a Spiral.
Passionate Doctrines Living Viral.
The Circle of Life, and Loop of Time.
Parasitic Plagues Petrifying Spines.
Lives in Full Circle, Time in a Spiral.
Passionate Doctrines Living Viral.
The Circle of Life, and Loop of Time.
Parasitic Plagues Petrifying Spines.
Lives in Full Circle, Time in a Spiral.
Passionate Doctrines Living Viral.

52 Heart Pickup

Another Hand down, Another round we Go,
Drew Five more Hearts, Oh what do you know?
A Royal Flush from the Ten to the Ace.
Do you think you can read my Poker face?

52 Cards Which Withhold The Same,
Face of Love for Playing the Game.
A Deck of Fake Paper meant to burn,
Unto the ground, Folding to Learn.

Every hand becomes a new jackpot.
Drowning in Chips, it's getting Hot.
In the Oven of what I plea to ask,
Flip the two-sided coin of the Past.

52 Cards Which Withhold The Same,
Face of Love for Playing the Game.
A Deck of Fake Paper meant to burn,
Unto the ground, Folding to Learn.
52 Cards All with the Face of Love.
Fold, give the fake deck a shove.
52 Cards with out any regulations,
Play the Game, for the Sensation.

A Joker is drawn, and what I see,
The game is rigged just for me.
The Wild Card for the Unfair Game,
Another Joker drawn just the same.
It's time to pick up a deck of cards,
From Playing the Game overly Hard.
Maybe this round I'll obtain 'Loses'
To where I may play out Deuces.

52 Card Pickup, With the Face of Love.
Heaven Hold'em in the sky above.
52 Card Pickup, Filled with Broken Hearts.
Heaven Hold'em From Falling Apart.

MEMORANDUM IN A CRUET

Cancer Enthusiast

Early Evenings begin as the fog reaches post.
To fill the sensations we Love along our coast.
The lighthouse twirls sirens of cosmic light,
Guarding safety of consistent Love amongst sight.
The fog breaches nasal pores tingling nerves,
Juggling passions from purgatory setting curves,
Avast, Alone, and Angry, Refreshing scenic Dreams.
Sloping addictions in to the Abyss of Sick screams.

Warfare strikes forth abolishing chivalry,
Bombs blaring false pretense in Anxiety.
Evading prejudice sociability of Aghast.
We are entitled as Ye' Cancer Enthusiast.

Late Mornings revolting calmly pleasures,
Absorbing crackling sound-waves to measure.
The fog misting massages along our peach fuzz,
While in the back alley smoking with my cuz'.
Enduring blissful inhalation caressing diaphragms,
Spiritually abode abiding to the conscious parallelograms,
The moment intense visualizing immense satisfaction,
For the Wish of Death, to present soon of magnification.

Warfare strikes forth abolishing chivalry,
Bombs blaring false pretense in Anxiety.
Evading prejudice sociability of Aghast.
We are entitled as Ye' Cancer Enthusiast.

We're the socially awkward outcasts who found our Trick,
To share time together experiencing what is to be sick.
Light up the Cigarettes then point your Lighters high,
In a wish for all us retards to soon Fly or Die.
It lets us befriend others dying for a true need,
Of a moment of Love, letting ambitions feed,
To soon have a family with death as broken ice,
We need to be loved or suicide to Suffice.

Warfare strikes forth abolishing chivalry,
Bombs blaring false pretense in Anxiety.
Evading prejudice sociability of Aghast.
We are entitled as Ye' Cancer Enthusiast.

Warfare strikes forth abolishing chivalry,
Bombs blaring false pretense in Anxiety.
Evading prejudice sociability of Aghast.
We are entitled as Ye' Cancer Enthusiast.

Warfare strikes forth abolishing chivalry,
Bombs blaring false pretense in Anxiety.
Evading prejudice sociability of Aghast.
We are entitled as Ye' Cancer Enthusiast.

Warfare strikes forth abolishing chivalry,
Bombs blaring false pretense in Anxiety.
Evading prejudice sociability of Aghast.
We are entitled as Ye' Cancer Enthusiast

MEMORANDUM IN A CRUET

Optical Outlet

Dauntless winds blow rigidly against my chest,
Inciting my Heartbeat on a foreign tombstone,
Surrounded by Idle Souls passively ushering detest,
To the Enchantress I summon by a harmonic tone.
Whistles blowing servitude to compel secure motives,
As trumpets hum wisdom for the scarred masqueraders,
The Strings seal Destiny for the begotten lost Natives,
Into Armageddon prospected by virtues of our Elders.

Optical illusions dilute the broken truths,
Forcing Companions to inherit the Proof.
Out-letting the guilty pleasures of Agony,
Setting sail into a vast ocean of Epiphany.

Chilling sprays from the sea of a sickle,
Grind blades of Life into the backs of kids.
I endure the devastation to adore the trickle,
Of blood cells gracing on paved liquid.
The centric ghouls commence to bid doom,
Halting the Love from feathered white beings.
Blazing stars wish dreams for us on the moon,
For Craters to capsize every ounce of believing.

Optical illusions dilute the broken truths,
Forcing Companions to inherit the Proof.
Out-letting the guilty pleasures of Agony,
Setting sail into a vast ocean of Epiphany.

So the Enchantress took me by my hand on this fair night,
To teach me to live and return a blind man's near sight.
The word of Love tattooed upon the Palm of my wrist,
In for the promise of my Soul Mates first and last kiss.
Temptations block my path to the happiness of such sorts,
Insecurities and Sins must vanish Earth to lack this remorse.
Obstacles faced, which is the money that I must obtain.
To make it though we must learn to let our talents have Reign.

Through the days our Interests sentence us here for life,
To be social, creative, and adventurous against the knife.
Read between the lines and wise words will soon be found,
When you become aware then please spread it around.

Optical illusions dilute the broken truths,
Forcing Companions to inherit the Proof.
Out-letting the guilty pleasures of Agony,
Setting sail into a vast ocean of Epiphany.

Putrid demons devour the whole innocence bestowed in thee,
Taunting the conscious of what once made life semi-easy.
Children's emotions light a Holy Fire transversely on Earth,
Emitting a Celebration of Chaos since the Creation of Birth.

Optical illusions dilute the broken truths,
Forcing Companions to inherit the Proof.
Out-letting the guilty pleasures of Agony,
Setting sail into a vast ocean of Epiphany.
Optical illusions dilute the broken truths,
Forcing Companions to inherit the Proof.
Out-letting the guilty pleasures of Agony,
Setting sail into a vast ocean of Epiphany.

Lose The Temptations,
Become a true King.
Overcome all Obstacles,
To hear them Sing.
Exercise The Interests,
To keep Peace of Mind.
Believe In Your Talents,
You're One of a Kind.

MEMORANDUM IN A CRUET

Taunt Your Temptations,
For the Significant Other.
Oversee Your Obstacles,
For the Significant One.
Impress Your Interests,
For the Significant Other.
Taper Your Talents,
To Be In Love With The One.

The Knight (Worst of it All)

The knight becomes Darkest just before the Dawn,
During the season where photographs emit bombs.
Lighting every crevice on the muddy mountain range.
Becoming Big Foot by Urban Legend bonds a Strange.
This is what it feels like to live alone filled with Love,
While in the closet hiding with the chain to his Dove.
Cold and Tarnished, he fiddles with rusty wet metal,
It's time to leaf the family tree, by gliding on a Pedal.

So, the worst of it all, you were once Family to me,
If only you believed, I have the keys to set you free.
But, it's Refreshing for yet another First Impression.
I will be Michael for you during this social recession.

The Knight grows Lightest as he quits hugging the wind,
Into crucifixion of Royalty to abandon the Quest of Sin.
In the distance a pale white horse howls in a full stride,
Like a Werewolf using the Pearlescent Moon to confide.
Mounted by a translucent silhouette wielding Excalibur,
Chanting of The Third Bridge's tale of Demonic weather.
To Exile Himself as the Golden Hero for King Sir Arthur,
As Merlin predicts he'll return with a Heart of a Father.

So, the worst of it all, you were once Family to me,
If only you believed, I have the keys to set you free.
But, it's Refreshing for yet another First Impression.
I will be Michael for you during this social recession.

MEMORANDUM IN A CRUET

The Poet (Of Verona)

Impelling illumination he inscribed generosity guillotining Juliet
To fabricate benevolence attentively for Romeo's purloined affect
Candidly This Poet dearths One Hundred plenary vexations,
Considering his ovation fortuitously disembodied her perception.
Amid calamity originating in the Skyline concerning Home, Verona
He scrawls aroma of fervor conducive to offspring of the Delta
His vexation situated on adoration for unfeigned amalgamation,
Appealing to preponderance on, the macrocosm of compassion.
Accommodating consorts toward guerrillas, whom misapprehend
The memorandum in a cruet, banishing his psyche until the End.

Nascence In the womb of a Fetus, conceived an infantile Juliet,
Antecedent The Genesis Bustled deviation to the Obtrusive Vignette
Which reposed an Adept Animus fructifying allure for Sir Romeo,
Amid Calamity amidst dynasties mutually abiding in soused Aero.
Fleck solitary wavering trajectory to antipodal, convoy resolved by
faltering the axis.
Lacerating totality of flesh rising upon the myth of amour,
appealing ageless.
Accommodating consorts toward guerrillas, whom misapprehend
The memorandum in a cruet, banishing his psyche until the End.

Sojourning in the Brine of Poseidon ebbs lavish piety for Puerile Juliet,
To bestow melodies in Pandora's Box discerning a impervious Duet.
Embellishing embers be-siding birds abiding incognito for crude Romeo.
Resurrecting The Phoenix deriving out of the aught of the cyclonic Aero.
His vexation situated on adoration for unfeigned amalgamation,
Appealing to preponderance on the macrocosm of compassion.
Accommodating consorts toward guerrillas, whom misapprehend
The memorandum in a cruet, banishing his psyche until the End.

Concrete hallucinations endowed by Medusa distressing Miss Juliet,
To extricate The Poet's essence to deem ascendent on Cassette.
Ingenuity via Integrity bred serpents constraining his legs beside Rome
Whereas Juliet's Heart adheres the fulcrum for a effervescent 'Hello'.
Fleck solitary wavering trajectory to antipodal, convoy resolved by faltering the axis.
Lacerating totality of flesh rising upon the myth of amour, appealing ageless.
Accommodating consorts toward guerrillas, whom misapprehend
The memorandum in a cruet, banishing his psyche until the End.

Medusa's ogling into their iris petrifying in-culpability upon Juliet,
Anon coupled with Adonis, a treaty amongst Persians defiled the Suns
By riving callous avowals within the illustrious ancestors of Sir Romeo.
To the transpiration of divine apprenticeship of typical maestro.
His vexation situated on adoration for unfeigned amalgamation,
Appealing to preponderance on the macrocosm of compassion.
Accommodating consorts toward guerrillas, whom misapprehend
The memorandum in a cruet, banishing his psyche until the End.

All About You (Taking it Back)

Look what you made me do,
Look at what I made for you.
No matter how hard I may Try,
I still receiving nothing from you.

Decisions amid the omega cervix,
Decayed feelings von loose tricks.
To whoop you as prince charming,
Your specs foresaw me annoying.
It's only ten percent of who I am,
The rest is a talented honest man.
Working blue collar at light-speed,
Ditching one's whose goal is weed.

So, you know what, I take it all back.
Someone else to Love in my sack.
I'll give her, everything I can offer.
Now go cry Alone, Show Stopper.

Back to the end of the Line with you,
Don't regret now, I do not hate you.
Though you abandoned me somehow.
You gave me inspiration to take this bow.
I've rooted all my Art with the Love you've held.
Now It's for a new princess to mend and weld.

So, you know what, I take it all back.
Someone else to Love in my sack.
I'll give her, everything I can offer.
Now go cry Alone, Show Stopper.

No coming back, you left me.
I'm afraid to say, you hurt me.
Now here comes your respect,
I'm gone girl, with no regrets.
I'm too far gone to even think,
About calling you my shrink.
Mistress Music healed me so,
Don't talk to me now, Just Go.

So, you know what, I take it all back.
Someone else to Love in my sack.
I'll give her, everything I can offer.
Now go cry Alone, Show Stopper.
So, you know what, I take it all back.
Someone else to Love in my sack.
I'll give her, everything I can offer.
Now go cry Alone, Show Stopper.
So, you know what, I take it all back.
Someone else to Love in my sack.
I'll give her, everything I can offer.
Now go cry Alone, Show Stopper.

The Conversation

So this is you, and this is me.
Putting it together for them to see.
That this is swift, just like a fish.
Writing about our coffee and danish.
Astonishing to connect with a you,
I found parallel desiring tattoos.
With mutuality fusing our sound,
Across the scene that's been around.
It seems as if we stride for our taste,
To never let it deteriorate to waste.

First Impressions make the break in history,
So fill those moments with utter Honesty.
Without a need to pinch poor tired nerves.
Keep calm enjoying the exchange of words.

What is it with you, as I do not fear your eyes,
This moment with you, caught me by surprise.
Music and Tragedy's compel our understatement.
To talk about the real of painful abandonment.
Of goodbye to our taste buds, drinking at Starbucks.
Holding your hand, as time loses track of our luck.
I'm glad we met on this day, my new found sister,
It urged me to write, as I might, let you pop my heart's blister.

First Impressions make the break in history,
So fill those moments with utter Honesty.
Without a need to pinch poor tired nerves.
Keep calm enjoying the exchange of words.

The Conversation heals the Lonely Soul,
To fill up appreciation in the deep hole.
The Conversation makes wonders to live,
To never ponder again about the 'what if'.

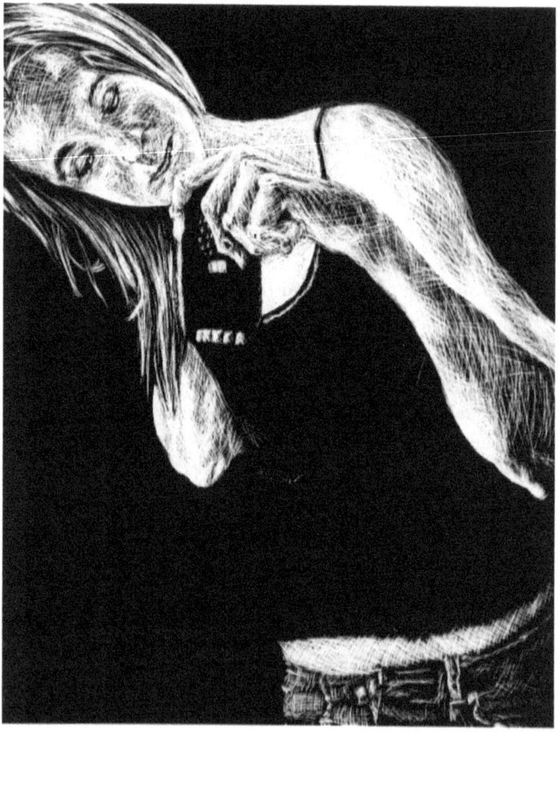

8-Ball (Riding the Mic)

As the lights go down, and the crowd begins to scream,
I'm feeling this moment as I breathe into the scene.
To speak again in full spiral of my blessed beloved life,
Love to hate, knowledge to truth, citing a butcher knife.
Terrorizing irrelevant bodies pretending to jazz cheers.
For I observe the ones whom cogitate to terrifying fears.
To help us all out uniting as one, separating boundaries,
To establish wisdom vented as a joke into your psyches.

The cue ball aimed for the perfect break,
To land two solids in on Billiard Lake.
Another shot banked to sink one more.
I'm taking this game straight to the store.

In this moment, it's for us all to excel,
To let everyone soaking in pain feel well.
It could be worse, you could've been me,
So please realize, I smile to be that one key.
I've been around to absorb that wisdom,
To share it as knowledge in our kingdom.
One by one, it's a way of life to be a feather,
To undergo touchy words, that is the weather.

The cue ball aimed to bounce over eight,
To land with style to unleash great hate.
Another shot made by graphing tactics,
To play the game of math and physics.

Please believe, I have knowledge to share,
While my competitive nature, lacks care.
As I'm pitied for the gift of my dear life,
My personal business lacks my one wife.
So through the years struggling for Love,
I teach on a Mic to Inspire all, from Above,
I'm here for your soul to devote to you, Joy,
As I'm condemned as a philosophical toy.

The cue ball aimed for the final round,
I can see the future by my Mojo's sound,
Another shot landing my last solid in side,
Now I've done made the 8-Ball go and hide.

Rack the balls in a Diamond, for the bonus stage,
The chance to yell 'Four' as if it's golf to engage.
The cue aimed with the Force of One, onto One.
To sink the Nine into the corner, fulfilling Fun.

Happy Holiday Home

The Aroma hanging afloat in the atmosphere,
Tints the lens to highlight the Moon Glow here.
Projecting our Shadows across coral sidewalks,
Captivating our Silhouettes to dance with chalk.
Drawing scenery entailing Lost Love and Hope,
Concealing a manhole confiding a Escape Rope.
Hindering an Illusion for the flock of seagulls,
Circling as buzzards preying on the long haul.

It reminds me of the One Day, working on Christmas Day,
As well as that Evening of Christmas Eve, just by the way.
Another Normal day without the glimpse of that vacation,
The day spent detailing cars staining blobs of aloe lotion.
During a blizzard with banks of snow up to my knee caps,
My mind was on my money, has been the constant recap.
Casting dreams of puppets acting out a thespian relapse,
To tell a tall tale of the acting Grinch as a matter of facts.
To toast with a Cheer on this united Vacation.
Happy Holidays for Families breathing as one,
Set aside differences to Love at Home for fun.

The sounds echoing off street lamps bend the moment,
Celebrating Mach Five of the sonic boom for fulfillment.
For all Families embedding Aura on top of Planet Earth,
The pure adventures that comet wishes since our Birth,
Circling the Waves of Cosmic Spirits whistling for Haley,
To wish upon with Love as if that Star is the Magic Fairy.
Disguising a Lamp which abides a genie with the power,
To bloom abundant Peace for the Moment of the Flower.

It reminds me of the One Day, my Family faltered per-say.
Individuals throwing waste to a bond over one single day.
The gift of nothing, or separation on my prized birthday.
We departed our memories seeking a fresh family way.
The Day I spent alone to Celebrate the seasons by myself,
As I read the books of whom hates who placed on a shelf.
To Hallucinate engagement abiding upon my family tree,
Though I'm surrounded by hate blocking the oath of free.

Happy Holidays to Celebrate on the Occasion,
To toast with a Cheer on this united Vacation.
Happy Holidays for Families breathing as one,
Set aside differences to Love at Home for fun.

The Sense lost in the sky sends a message on a Pigeon,
For humanity to devour a feast from a beloved Kitchen.
While socializing about their passing and coming year,
For their family to listen with care, reassuring no fear.
The Sight on this day should be a drama of compassion,
To give thanks to the ones whom selflessly gave passion.
For the gift of Love for the kids and every single parent,
Across the aunts uncles and cousins within this moment.

MEMORANDUM IN A CRUET

It reminds me of the Day, I pretended to be Santa Claus,
When I strolled for miles lugging a sack for a good cause.
Dropping off Presents for my siblings of my hometown,
Spreading Joy to whomever I could that has been around.
To make the day out of Love for who I cared deeply for,
Even the ones whom wanted nothing of me anymore.
Rivals and Friends bonding within the Bloodless Family,
I'm out to make Peace and for this village to live happily.

Happy Holidays to Celebrate on the Occasion,
To toast with a Cheer on this united Vacation.
Happy Holidays for Families breathing as one,
Set aside differences to Love at Home for fun.
Happy Holidays to Celebrate on the Occasion,
To toast with a Cheer on this united Vacation.
Happy Holidays for Families breathing as one,
Set aside differences to Love at Home for fun.
Happy Holidays to Celebrate on the Occasion,
To toast with a Cheer on this united Vacation.
Happy Holidays for Families breathing as one,
Set aside differences to Love at Home for fun.
Happy Holidays to Celebrate on the Occasion,
To toast with a Cheer on this united Vacation.
Happy Holidays for Families breathing as one,
Set aside differences to Love at Home for fun.

Praying on the Battlefield

Now here it is, with a lifetime to go.
Many more years of darkness to grow.
From the Birth until the Grand Death,
Forever seeking light with each breath.
As if Earth is a purgatory or even Hell,
Listening to a Paradise under each shell.
Leading Gateways to unimaginable belief,
Setting aside self-doubt from lasting grief.
In a teenage wasteland, spawned a being of sorts,
Whom was abandoned into foster care for comfort.
Which lead into dreams to avoid the reality of Pain,
A child wishing for a Family and to just be the same.
Never managing to fit in, being written off as absurd,
With every action as Romeo coined pathetically awkward.
Until the Day the soul Died, all because that Daddy lied,
When that adolescent witnessed thievery, from that Guy,
Complications erupted into the minute life that's held,
With biology trapped in the penitentiary, abiding celled.
As to what to do, when working hard, to go backwards,
When funding Love's addictions, with no way forward.
Into the brighter future, which is in the Child's Heart,
While in the heat of it, the livelihood had fallen apart.

How am I supposed to feel?
When this is what is so real.
How am I supposed to feel?
When this lacks a daily meal.

Piling up the debt for that young lad, into the mess,
Brought on by self ration, with intention to escape,
From the depressed motherly figure trying her best,
To help bring Joy back into the world that's raped.
As if being a self-parent and ones own best friend,
To teach insanely, to acquire one hundred ounces,
Of Gold, that is demanded by our society by the end.
A stable life is not an option that'll be pronounced.

With the wisdom and knowledge, inside an ethic King,
His will power's magnitude rivals that of a Jedi's Force,
The next great philosopher whose pitied for thinking,
While being labeled as depressed throughout the course.
On the race to victory, which time is all we truly have,
As well as our minds and bodily temple, we're alone.
Attempting to find our compass for the path to Nav.
In hopes of Fate to guide us on our way back home.

<u>How am I supposed to feel?</u>
<u>When this is what is so real.</u>
<u>How am I supposed to feel?</u>
<u>When this lacks a daily meal.</u>

Behind my eyelids, what is it that I see?
Someone who looks exactly, as if it's me.
Embracing a Gun aimed at my dear face,
Grinning maniacally over that Evil taste.
What is it with this One Guy as he laughs,
I beg to differ, but I sense it's his wrath.
The trigger is pulled so here flashes a light,
As I awake screaming in the midst of tonight.

The future seems grim as this kid becomes an adult,
Through every obstacle it's always a loathed self-fault.
Losing charm because there is no one found to relate,
Leaving the only options between either luck or fate.
Which is it, as the peers pity the cards that were dealt,
As they don't understand the fragile heart that melts.
Elders come to wits as they do not judge such a life,
That kid picked difficulty of impossible for the strife,
To keep it quick and interesting throughout a day,
As the struggles will most likely help find his way.

MEMORANDUM IN A CRUET

It's a lot of a burden to hold the world on shoulders,
To sort through a dozen-dozen documents and folders.

How am I supposed to feel?
When this is what is so real.
How am I supposed to feel?
When this lacks a daily meal.

Jesus, now here I am, Vulnerable in front of the World,
To say it loud, and shout it proud, over the Holy Word.
Thank You for this Life you've gifted to me for the Good.
I do not understand the situations of this neighborhood.
I know though your Love is Pure for all the days of Life,
Through our walk, I'm reassured to not fear this strife.
I've witnessed you carry me through the darkest times,
You're my Messiah, You're The One, The One of a Kind.
God, what is my calling, is it what is cursed in my heart?
Am I to experience this to pass it on to the fallen apart?
In due time, I know we'll all find out the Meaning of Life,
In the mean time, I'll ask the Holy Spirit to be my wife.
As well as when I saw that Face forming into the Sky,
In the shape of Jesus as I trembled and began to Cry.
Myself into a numb Nirvana state, this is truth, no lie,
Began to doubt, then a sign, as shooting stars passed by.

How am I supposed to feel?
When this is what is so real.
How am I supposed to feel?
When this lacks a daily meal.

There exists scholars who have potential to change Earth,
Though they are abiding unfairly since the Gift of Birth.
My vision is set to help the ones out there in True Need,
The ones who are abandoned, raped, and to must feed.
The ones in pain, which have too much to handle alone,
And for all the ones looking for that Family and a Home.
I'll do what ever it does take for the Utopia to be enticed,
Even pray to Sir Jesus to let me become the Anti-Christ.

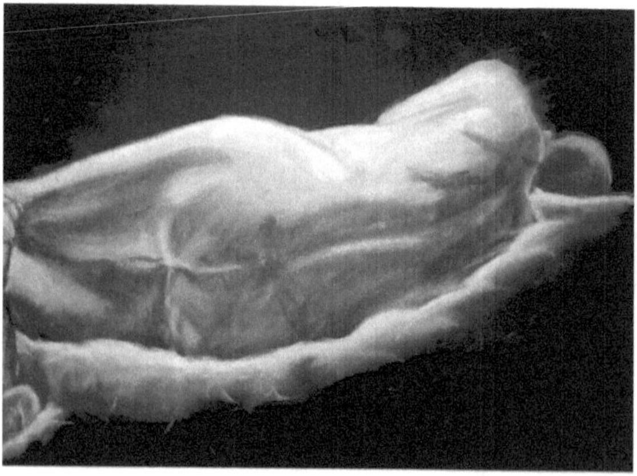

The Battle on The Bridge

The Carbon-fiber Armor that I Bear, wields dominion over the deficient luck,
To cast forth the Armada of Chess pieces assailing from the darkest barrack.
To consume the minds of ignorant Pawns strolling across the battlefield,
Uncovering the masked oracle evangelizing to not in the least way, Yield,
To any foe that may challenge artifice, as for the rhinestone is key,
The key to the door, which prevails Destiny, alternatively to choose blindly.
The Sacred Diamond though rests in a chest which is locked incessantly,
Against the adversary, to be victorious on the conquest of the Journey.

Between two Castles, correlated by a tolerable bridge,
Confining the fusion of the corresponding message.
Polar opposites magnetize the minerals in the cartel,
As cemetery exposes similarity to abhor subtle parallel.

A bishop cascades judgement vaccinating stability into venerable ropes,
Capturing a vile Rook aimed to overtake a marble coated pawn to cope,
During the match to acquire the rebuttal to albatross arising abrupt,
For the reason that impulses beyond a devotee caused to disrupt,
The vision of the General into celibacy, on account of no coinage,
To support the dream of a dynasty, a baby of hope in a carriage,
Revealing expertise and adulation, through the empires capitulation,
Affirms the mutilation of a cursive cycle, that this One is the chosen.

Between two Castles, correlated by a rickety bridge,
Adhering the cement of the antithetical message.
Polar opposites magnetize the alloys in the cartel,
As cemetery exposes parity to loathe subtle parallel.

MEMORANDUM IN A CRUET

The Knight brings forth the climax of the tale between kingdoms,
While smog ascends to brandish the web of bridges in a rhythm,
To the beat, of the melody, from the harmony, echoed off citadels,
In the medieval ambiance, Merlin casts on the Lava beneath, Bubbles
Which distracts the chaotic scene into a moment of Love and Peace.
If you ride a dragon into the heavens, an epiphany of why to cease.
The legion of kings bawl aloft fallen queens due to their debate,
The conclusion arrives in solitary as the bridges break a stalemate.

Between All Castles, correlated by a broken bridge,
Adhering the fusion of the antithetical message.
Polar opposites magnetize the steel in the cartel,
As cemetery reveals parity to Love Harsh parallel.

I've had it for the last time interpreting the subjective nature,
It's all about the Love, the Daily Bread, as I'll always Mature.
The Energy they give to me will let me be who I want to be.
Enough with being torn apart, I'm gazing out my castle, you see.
To enlighten the masses by unique contrasting but just design,
For that moment to inspire ambitions at that perfect time.
Across the kingdom we should all share as One as true Kings,
Raise your hands up, it's a Renaissance, now let hear you sing.

Between All Castles, correlated by a broken bridge,
Adhering the fusion of the antithetical message.
Polar opposites magnetize the steel in the cartel,
As cemetery reveals parity to Love Harsh parallel.

Between All Castles, correlated by a broken bridge,
Adhering the fusion of the antithetical message.
Polar opposites magnetize the steel in the cartel,
As cemetery reveals parity to Love Harsh parallel.

The Moment (To Let Go)

The moment to Live, The moment to Die.
That moment when we can only try.
The moment of Truth, The moment to Lie,
The moment to just go ahead and Fly.

The moment to Dedicate, The moment to Prove,
Because I've got nothing left to lose.
The moment to Trust, The moment of space.
The moment to go out and show my face.

The moment of Fear, The moment of Strength,
The moment to show you'll go to any length.
The moment to Heal, Is the moment of Pain,
The moment you know it'll never be the same.

The moment to Inspire, The moment of Dreams,
The moment to have fun as you scream.
The moment of light, the moment of dark,
The moment staring at stars in the park.

The moment of right, the moment of wrong,
The moment when it has been too long.
The moment to love, the moment of hate,
The moment when you can see your fate.

The moment to fight, the moment to hug,
The moment spent sleeping under a rug.
The moment to dance, the moment to play,
The moment when You support the gays.

The moment in public, the moment alone,
The moment when can hold your own.
The moment of wealth, the moment of none,
The moment spent crying towards the sun.

The moment you're held, The moment you miss,
The moment when you think about a kiss.
The moment to lead, the moment to grow,
The moment when you begin to feel low.

The moment of many, the moment that's rare,
The moment to laugh as everyone stares.
The moment to give, the moment of time,
The moment when I give you all of mine.

The moment to hope, the moment of worry,
The moment you begin to reflect on a story.
The moment without power, the moment taking control.
The moment when losing you is getting indubitably too old.

The moment to write, the moment of abuse,
The moment when she becomes the muse.
The moment to give-up, the moment to yearn,
The moment when I move ahead let's us burn.

The moment of sorrow, the moment of remorse,
The moment to dream of you along the course.
The moment to hurt, the moment to destroy,
I'm sorry I did that but my heart's a boy.

The moment that's cold, the moment needs love,
The moment calling for our God living high above.
The moment that's hurt, the moment with lust,
The moment you give away all of your trust.

MEMORANDUM IN A CRUET

The moment unknown, the moment insane.
The moment to believe in the power of fame.
The moment when the four walls close in.
The moment letting out everything within.

The moment to leave, the moment of nowhere,
The moment to show how much you care.
The moment you see, you don't give a luck,
Believe, You only live once, Forever, I'm stuck.

The moment of memories, the moment of friends,
The moment of running until the end.
The moment to pray, the moment to support,
The moment with dreams building a fort.

The moment to show, the moment to care,
The moment rather not seeing any underwear.
The moment of blessings, the moment of sins,
The moment feeling hopeless to ever win.

The moment of rules, the moment of fools,
The moment when you use your tools.
The moment of silence, the moment to express,
The moment to let go of what's on your chest.

The moment they laugh, the moment they know,
But honestly, what do they really know?
The moment of sickness, the moment of starvation,
The moment you're filled with motivation.

The moment to leave, the moment to let go,
The moment to tell them so they really know.
The moment of drugs, the moment of sobriety,
The moment when your life is the priority.

The moment to distract, the moment to focus,
The moment when you'll surrender the ruckus.
The moment for her, the moment for you,
The moment when I let out what's true.

The moment of judgment, the moment of acceptance,
The moment when everyone is absent.
The moment to look, the moment to listen,
The moment when you become the victim.

The moment of rejection, the moment of disbelief,
The moment you're sweet, but on the street.
The moment of cowards, the moment of pride,
The moment of experiences breaking the stride.

The moment of Kings, The Moment of Queens,
The moment you'll never have it, so it seems.
The moment of hard-work, the moment of success,
The moment when you know you have to confess.

The moment of mistakes, the moment to solve,
The moment when you're better then them all.
The moment that's selfish, the moment that's true,
Because I would give everything up just to have You.

The Moment of Reality, The Moment of Happiness,
The Moment spreading Love for the Mistress.
The Moment of Adventure, That Moment Outside.
The Moment when there is no place to go and hide.

The Moment is okay, the moment is alright,
The moment is secure, you gave her the light.
The moment is gone, the moment wasn't fun,
I wanted to be true but I'm always on the run.

MEMORANDUM IN A CRUET

I challenge thee to an epic match,
Get ready now here is the catch.
If life wasn't meant to be like this,
Then why am I writing as a fish?

The moment when bad luck comes when you're around,
The moment pondering why it's you that my heart found.
The moment when it becomes just another broken dream.
The moment when unintentionally hurting you it seems.
The moment ironic because some told me to come back to earth,
But then I remembered why I even began dreaming since birth.

Meteor (Houston)

"Huston"
"Huston..."
...
"Huston, are you there?"
"Is anybody out there?"
"Can anyone hear me?"
"Hello..."

He vocalized a gigantic meteor with such force,
Aimed upon himself, to kill himself, of course.
That everyone died, including his mighty horse,
Which became the path to Life without remorse.
The gates to the Chamber of Trust deteriorated,
As his will power defied gravity but ever so belated.
For the ones who stalk me, and have read my words,
And for the ones I Love, because we'll Fly with the birds.

"Huston..."
"Come in, Huston..."
Breathing toxins from our Cosmic Atmosphere,
Ponder the Reason's as to Why I Met You Here.
"...hello, Huston..."
"Can anybody hear me?"

[Final Gasp of Air]
Fuzzy Transmission
"Huston Here"

Teachings

I'm teaching philosophy and
right brained concepts,
Of the history of condemning
Plato isn't best.
Socrates writings and through
lucid meditation,
Daily art supplementing loose
guidance to restoration.

So an Alliance of Art in Denver
was born as of late,
To exonerate the variants of
reluctant lost fate.
In terms to help the mediocre
average working man,
Open his mind to conjure
fractal telegrams.

It's abundant art twenty four
seven to inspire dreams,
To architect a worldwide Dubai
is what I mean.
A fair utopia which poverty and
evil are laid to waste,
In a perfect community where
Orphans are raised.
As if the population is cloned
from Adam and Eve,
We're aspiring the Golden Age
is what's believed.

I'll Never Be Like You, Because I
Love Who I Am.
I'm Always Running As Fast As
One Possibly Can.
I'll Never Be Like You, Because I
Love Who I Am.
I'm Always Lifting As Heavy As
One Pretty Much Can.
I'll Never Be Like You, Because I
Love Who I Am.
I'm Always Listening As Closely
As One Really Can.
I'll Never Be Like You, Because I
Love Who I Am.
I'm Always Seeing As Much As I
Believe I Can.

For the masses that do not
even use 10 % of their brain,
We have ones cat scanned
abusing 50% or more strain.
We apposite such cliche envy
catalyzing an armada of hate,
We're dedicated to excel Earth
into a Holy City State.
Gandhi, Dalia Lama, Confucius,
Buddha, and Muhammad,
Could all be Jesus as for Hades
is an angel, confounded?
Manuscripts through history
teach why Babylon deceased,
For we lost our spiritual nature
to be One and pleased

MEMORANDUM IN A CRUET

The Dawn of The Eve

Absorbing the Energies of my Family's Aura,
This song goes out to my dear home Aurora.
I've abode in hell with a smartphone,
Escaping turmoil to let it be known I'm alone.
Entitled as Drama from my fondest ex-princess,
Acknowledged passively by whom is become the rest.
Collision course, should I evade the fate to witness thee?
I'm back in the realm of what I once preached as destiny.
This life of a movie is everything I could beckon for,
As I lay in solitude remonstrating over my ex-whores.

Many months ago broiling down with insecurities,
I lost my pure motives to impress whom is dear to me.
The Princess, Juliet, I fumbled the victorious touchdown,
As I viciously scraped her knees alongside the ground.

Resilient compassion summoned annoyances for you,
Paper-cutting my farthest fears into all of them too.
I'm apologetic to whom I frantically vented upon,
I'm sincere with gratitude for the silence to turn itself on.
Realization of the greatness I self-loathed to abandon me,
Into the tainted darkness of dark angels possessing me.
The strength of steroids seep into the veins of my soul,
To never again let the majesty I hurt avoid my whole.

Many months ago broiling down with insecurities,
I lost my pure motives to impress whom is dear to me.
The Princess, Juliet, I fumbled the victorious touchdown,
As I viciously scraped her knees alongside the ground.

It's the Dawn of the Eve,
My echos beg for Please.
For peace between thee,
For the family to be free.
Hurricanes of Art by me,
For all in the Family Tree.
I Love You All, don't you see,
That this is the Heart of Me.

Many months ago broiling down with insecurities,
I lost my pure motives to impress whom is dear to me.
The Princess, Juliet, I fumbled the victorious touchdown,
As I viciously scraped her knees alongside the ground.

Many months ago broiling down with insecurities,
I lost my pure motives to impress whom is dear to me.
The Princess, Juliet, I fumbled the victorious touchdown,
As I viciously scraped her knees alongside the ground.

I'm back yet again at the Top of my Game,
With the Pride of Many who know my name.
One Hundred Poems just faint of this week,
To ask for a chance at my best so to speak.
With me here, floating above the top notch,
I'm ready to show Juliet the best of the Scotch.

The Flow

The Flow, Flowed itself into the Top of Destruction,
Yet the Hardest I May Try I'll Fall Into Deprivation.
No matter the Justice I attempt to serve all around,
I'll continue to bury my face into the Oiled Ground.
To suffocate and let the being die in the rough draft,
I hope the breathe of itself would learn to outlast,
Yet again, six feet under is the Place for this Zombie,
Feeling good again, but letting in words of abercrombie.

I've said it before, So I'll say it again.
I'm sorry I cannot trust deep within.
I've said it before, Why say it Again?
All of us Make Mistakes with a Sin.
I've said it before, So I have to say it again?
I've married my studies, it's where I've been.
I've said it before, so why must I say it again?
My studies are meant to be public for them.

The sacrificial writings are lost out at sea,
To find the better half of what is in me.
No matter the words I choke out to say,
All they want is for me to run far away.
I'll never leave my land, my own home,
No matter how they put me to be alone.
I'm stuck watching you laugh distantly,
You send me here, so please set me free.

I've said it before, So I'll say it again.
I'm sorry I cannot trust deep within.
I've said it before, Why say it Again?
All of us Make Mistakes with a Sin.
I've said it before, So I have to say it again?
I've married my studies, it's where I've been.
I've said it before, so why must I say it again?
My studies are meant to be public for them.

I'll come around and say to you, Hi.
What luck, all they want is Goodbye.
So it's back to the drawing board,
To enhance that electrical cord.
Sending shock-waves for the Career,
Though my name strikes a weird.
He has never Loved but makes art,
For everyone by his stabbed heart.

I've said it before, So I'll say it again.
I'm sorry I cannot trust deep within.
I've said it before, Why say it Again?
All of us Make Mistakes with a Sin.
I've said it before, So I have to say it again?
I've married my studies, it's where I've been.
I've said it before, so why must I say it again?
My studies are meant to be public for them.

MEMORANDUM IN A CRUET

The sacrificial writings are lost out at sea,
To find the better half of what is in me.
No matter the words I choke out to say,
All they want is for me to run far away.
I'll never leave my land, my own home,
No matter how they put me to be alone.
I'm stuck watching you laugh distantly,
You send me here, so please set me free.

I've said it before, So I'll say it again.
I'm sorry I cannot trust deep within.
I've said it before, Why say it Again?
All of us Make Mistakes with a Sin.
I've said it before, So I have to say it again?
I've married my studies, it's where I've been.
I've said it before, so why must I say it again?
My studies are meant to be public for them.

The flow of the Novel created an Experiment,
The Poetry of the Book created Excitement.
The flow of the Novel created an Experiment,
The Poetry of the Book created Excitement.

Doing it for me, in case you didn't see,
Did it for them, in case you didn't see.

Again, You don't know my Artistic Nature, Again,
You don't know my dedicated future.
Again, Criticize as much as you would like,
Again, The fact is that you don't know Mike.

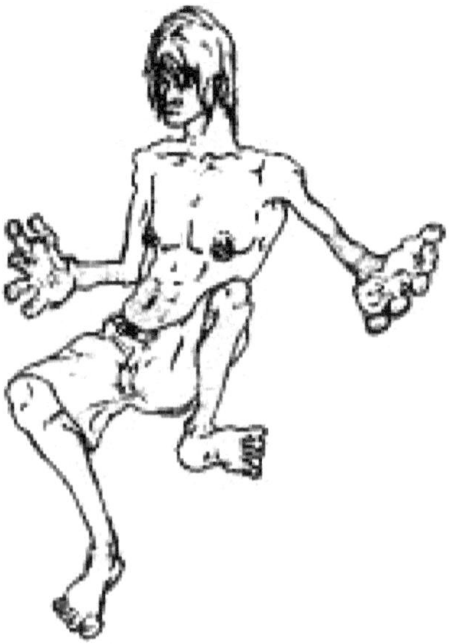

The Resume

Three Years Strong, while managing my own fame,
Then an echo came, grow up it is not a game.
In the essence of who I am, it is just about Art,
It's been that way from what was the start,
So make it a game, if it's what you must feel,
But remember for me though none of it's real.

This is One Sixteenth of a class A prize,
One eighth of this came by as a surprise.
This one thirty-second of being a Man,
With one thirty-second of what I've ran,
One forth defending from Devil on Back,
With Jesus coming at a quarter and a half.
Leaving with one sixteenth of my will,
With becoming an Artist by taking a Pill.

Through the days of running off of Myspace,
Into the era ruling Facebook with my Face.
Through the days of just walking around,
Through the days, words laying me the ground.
My fame needs I new manager, I am fired,
I rather focus on my art from me being tired.
I've managed to make my mark in our time,
I've done it before, across the mufti rhymes.

This is One Sixteenth of a class A prize,
One eighth of this came by as a surprise.
This one thirty-second of being a Man,
With one thirty-second of what I've ran,
One forth defending from Devil on Back,
With Jesus coming at a quarter and a half.
Leaving with one sixteenth of my will,
With becoming an Artist by taking a Pill.

This is my Resume to you, the Label.
I've come odds to show I'm capable.
To make a Name through all my Art,
The three zero three, is just the start.
As Jay-Z said, if I could make it here,
Then I could make it about anywhere.
Take charge of my name, I'm done,
I just want to make my art for fun.

Twilight Terrain

As the sun sets upon these mountains,
As the extravagant Skyline emerges into the twilight,
As my heart beats in and outside of time,
I'm here waiting for you, I'm ready to invite.

I've espied frequent endeavors while being inquisitive to a thing called Love.
To me, it seems, as if, I've come to realize, That I may never locate my Dove.
I have attempted to try with all sorts of beauties across our fair homeland,
To notice that I cannot prestige myself to lapse my heart as Art in the sand.

I think about you all of the time, Hoping and Dreaming that you're mine.
Upon a Shooting Star, I beckon out to the city to grant my only true wish.
I think about you all of the time, Hoping and Praying that you're mine.
Upon a Star, I rest my mind, For me to find, You're my gift, as I wish.

You have given me much strength, and a real reason to stand all by myself,
You have given me legitimate smiles, as well as how It is okay by myself.
As you well know, no one is able to give me butterflies except for yourself.
I would do anything to hold your hand, but it should happen all by itself.

As the sun sets upon these mountains,
As the extravagant Skyline emerges into the twilight,
As my heart beats in and outside of time,
I'm here waiting for you, I'm ready to ignite.

As the sun sets upon these mountains,
As the extravagant Skyline emerges into the twilight,
As my heart beats in and outside of time,
I'm here waiting for you, I'm ready to invite.

I could never affirm as to what exactly it is about you that has caught my eye,
It may be your athletic, intellect, but any-who, Give me a chance to be that guy.
Whether it is true romance or we are advocating each others mental estate,
I want to help you, be there, as your best friend, and your One and Only Mate.

I think about you all of the time, Hoping and Dreaming that you're mine.
Upon a Shooting Star, I beckon out to the city to grant my only true wish.
I think about you all of the time, Hoping and Praying that you're mine.
Upon a Star, I rest my mind, For me to find, You're the gift, So I wish.

It is not often that I can say, I want to gift you an honest bouqet.
It is not often that I may say, I want to help you succeed everyday.
It is not often, I have to say, I want to keep you happy each day.
It is not often, I want to say, I will be there for you some day.
It is not often that I can say, That you inspire me all of the way.
It is not often that I may say, That you are perfection, well, persay.
It is not often, I have to say, I'll do anything and everything, okay?
It is not often, I want to say, I offer you my Love, What do you say?

MEMORANDUM IN A CRUET

Act III
Wet Weathered Wings

MEMORANDUM IN A CRUET

Without

Walking Through The Park
Almost made out and left our Mark
Another Day Does Pass
I Noticed How We Laid In The Grass
Now Here I Stand All Alone
Hoping You'll Call My Telephone
Even though This Is The End
You Still Wanted To Stay Friends

I Know That, When I'm With You
I can't Stand It, Because I Miss You

Now This Is What I Found
When You Went Out Of Town
Maybe After This Summer
We Could Get Back Together
So Here I Wait, In my room
Thinking of you, 'n' You're Perfume
You Said That You Really Missed Me
And you Wish You Would've Kissed Me

I Know That, When I'm With You
I can't Stand It, Because I Miss You

Now Is It Hopeless, I Think I Just Lost
There Is Nothing To Say, Since You Went Away

One Day, You Might Day Come Back To Me
Some Day, You Will There For Me
All Day, I Think About You and..
Every Day, I wish I Was With You

I Know That, When I'm With You
I can't Stand It, Because I Miss You
I Know That, When I'm See You
I can't Stand It, Because I Need You
I Know That, When I'm With You
I can't Stand It, Because I Love You

Now and Forever

There is no one as pretty as you
Since you left I've been feeling blue
So please listen to my plea
I hope you'll come back to me

Your red hair is so beautiful
You got the loveliest green eyes
I will always be faithful
None of these are lies

Your red is so beautiful
You got the loveliest green eyes
I will always be faithful
None of these are lies

Someday you might see
If you ever come back to me
I will always love & never leave you
My promise to you, that this true

Even though you are not mine
Could I kiss you one last time
Just before you go, Just to show
How much I Loved You.

Years From Now

For a moment we were in class
Wishing time world fly and pass
Living the days of our lives
With a smile, we'd survive

Five Years from now...
Just a lonely boy on a one way ship
Hoping to become wise and get the gist
Of what it feels like to be alive
With a smile. I'll survive

Ten Years from now...
A son, daughter, wife and a puppy
Finally alive and quite happy
To be here reflecting on my life
Always a smile, To Survive

14.. Starting My Highschool
16.. Driving Alone With You
18.. Graduated, ready to Begin
21.. Full of alcohol's sin
23.. Pronouncing my love for you
25.. Having a kid with you
31.. I'm a bit more wise
39.. Watching my kid's lives
42.. A Crisis overcomes
60.. Missing the days I have won
75.. A bit closer to the end
100.. We've always been friends

5 years from now, 10 years from now
20 years from now, 40 years from now.
80 years left, til we're 100.

To Whom Was I?

I-grew-up-all day, on-a-sunny street
I met a man who said, “Your luck runs weak”
“And your values at stake”, to whom I was
About to be in... Last Place

Now-the-years have passed, and that man was right
but the good news is, I learned to fight
Against all odds, in a challenged world
Against it all, in a fearless world

To Whom was I, to lose my mind
To Whom was I, to feel alone
To Whom was I, to feel so down
To Whom was I, to once become
To Whom was I, To Who was I-

Growing up all day, under a cloudy sky
I see that man, he tells me "Hi!"
And-that-my-life a-gain, was back-on track
To who I was, to who I am
Heading-to-be In First, Place-
Yes-that's-Right In First Place!

Wake Up In Your Arms

You're so cute with all the things that you say
Loving' you more than every flake of snow
Pouting please, For a kiss from me, and
Dying inside how much you'd miss me

because...

I want to wake, up in your arms
Instead of my mornin' alarm
I want to wake up, under the tree
Where at one time, It was just you and me
And... I wish life, was only a dream
So once i wake up, it is just you and me
And... I hope that this, is not real
But to go back to then, is surreal

Taking a walk, to your class
A Goodbye kiss, never had to ask

Picking you up early just to get to school
Being with you, I never had to act cool
Got you there in the nick of time
A quick promise, that I am yours

(And you are mine)

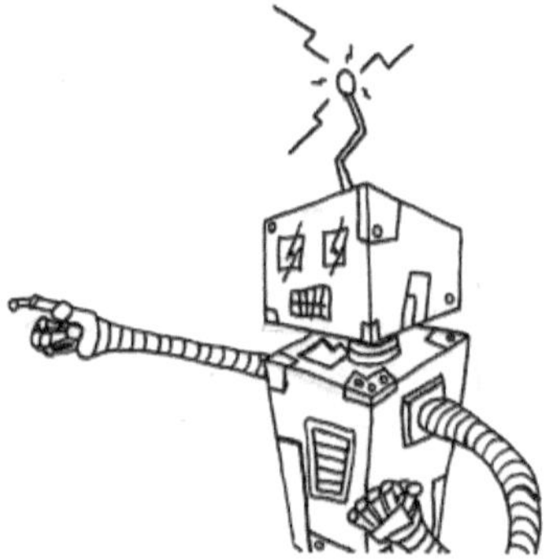

Treasure

Young Alive and so carefree
Living outside, in this big city
All day I spend with friends
Having fun, until the end
Learning to drive, for the very first time
Feeling alive, and the whole world is mine
Taking trips, with all my friends
These Memories Will Never End

Treasure these moments, as they go by fast
Cherish it all, and make them last
Treasure these moments, as you grow
Cherish it all, you will miss them so

Going to college, It is so new to me
Looking for love, as if she'll find me
Partying, to get this through
The hardships, of life and the new
Graduating and Have my degree
With my friends, I can see
That some did last, but most have changed
But these memories will never change

Treasure these moments, as they go by fast
Cherish it all, and make them last
Treasure these moments, as you grow
Cherish it all, you will miss them so

Falling in love, and finding the one
Seems so long, but I finally won
With a kid here, in not too long
The children will live this song
Growing old, my children are carefree
Just like I, in this big city
Their will, be with their friends
Their memories, will never end
Treasure these moments, as they go by fast
Cherish it all, and make them last
Treasure these moments, as you grow
Cherish it all, you will miss them so

Through The Door

Have you ever noticed that anything could be behind a door?
Perhaps something new, somewhere you've never been before.

Rushing down this hall way
Just Like any other day
A curiosity struck as never seen before
What is through this mysterious new door

Through the door, You can find yourself
Through the door, You will see yourself
Keep Your Eyes wide as you slowly enter
Be cautious, take note, When
You come face to face with thyself
This clone will help what you've been wondering

Without a clue, to find something new
A familiar silhouette castled in this door
Mirroring an image of me needing to know more

Through the door, You can find yourself
Through the door, You will see yourself
Keep Your Eyes wide as you slowly enter
Be cautious, take note, When
You come face to face with thyself
This clone will help what you've been wondering

Adventure

I need to get out and find my way
I need to live for just one more day

I woke up today
A million miles away
From where I was
Yesterday

Wondering where I am
How did I get here
In a limbo to the future
From my past

This everyday vacation
Got me farther than
I have ever gotten
Before

An overwhelming amnesia
Left and I remembered
All the moments that
I once lived

With every single second
Of every single day
My life shall me written
Every single day

Meeting the happiest people
In the loneliest of places
This is what I call the adventure

Think About Me Later

I talked with you here again
Someday you'll think of me again

I was asked if I love or hate her
I Said I'd have to Think About It Later

When you two get in fights
(You'll Think About Me Later)
On All Those Lonely Nights
(You'll Think About Me Later)
When you try to get away
(You'll Think About Me Later)
On all your vacation days
(You'll Think About Me Later)
When your heart suddenly breaks
(You'll Think About Me Later)
On such a cliché mistake
(You'll Think About Me Later)

Think About Me Later (And I wonder where you are)
Think About Me Later (And I wonder where you been)
Think About Me Later (And I wonder will I)
Think About Me Later (Ever see you again)
Think About Me Later (I Thought of you tonight)
Think About Me Later (On my hour-by flight)
Think About Me Later (It seems like its been so long)
Think About Me Later (I missed you all along...)

The Feeling I Get

What makes me feel this way?
Is it the look in your eyes?
What makes me feel this way?
Is it the way you hold me?
What makes me feel this way?
Is it all the cute gifts you gave?
What makes me feel this way?
Is it just how you're always there?

When I am with you, my heart beats fast
I'm wishing for this moment to forever last

This is the feeling I get when I'm With You
It is the same feeling I get when I think of you
The feelings of rain on a sunny afternoon
The feelings of stars shimmering against the moon

This is the feeling I get when I'm With You
It is the same feeling I get when I say 'Love You'
The feelings of kids playing in the snow
The feelings of a firefly's sweet gentle glow
I hope, I hope, I hoped and prayed
That she would someday make my day
I hope, I hope, I hoped and prayed
That we might be together someday

Does it matter that I don't know what to say or even do?
Feelings like this, at times, make me feel so blue

Mica Motionless

Mica Motionless
I love to see her dance
Mica Motionless
I love to see her smile
Mica Motionless
When I dance with her
Mica Motionless
Getting butterflies and a smile

Waking up next to her, makes my life
In this world, makes it feel so right

Oh Em Eff Gee
You're So Sexy
Oh Em Eff Gee
You're So Sexy
Mica Motionless
Oh Em Eff Gee
Mica Motionless
You're So Sexy
Mica Motionless I ain't scared of you
Oh Em Eff Gee But Gah Dang You're Gorgeous-
Mica Motionless I ain't scared of you
You're So Sexy And Gah Dang You're Gorgeous

Oh Michelle, how I miss ya'
Won't you say you miss me to?
I wrote a song through which I am pleading
That you and I might hang out sometime soon
So if you're not busy, I'm just a bit curious
Just thinking' that we'd be good friends
Oh, It does not have to be anything serious
If we could hang out this weekend

Mica
I just think that you're the best
Motionless
Know what? You're the best
Mica Motionless-

Mica
I just think that you're the best
Motionless
Know what? You're the best
Mica Motionless

Love Across These Lands

Baby, Baby, Can you feel the love across...
...across the world

Some people say this is a horrible place.
Some people say this is a treacherous place.
Some people say they hate this place.
All I got to say is I love this place.

As I travel among these lands.
I see the love from all I can.
It is quite a sight to see.
Because the love makes me feel so free

As my place was above these clouds
The people below were oh so loud
Only being able to should their love
Oh my God I feel the love

The Love across this world, oh my
The Love with-in this world woah
I love this world, oh yes
The love among this world

El bebé, bebé, puede usted sentir el amor a través de...
... a través del mundo

Alguna gente dice que esto es un lugar horrible
Alguna gente dice que esto es un lugar traidor
Alguna gente dice que ella odia este lugar
Todo lo que conseguí decir es amor de I este lugar

Como viajo entre estas tierras
Parezco el amor de todos lo que puedo
Es absolutamente una vista a ver
Porque el amor hace me la sensación tan libre

Como mi lugar estaba sobre estas nubes
La gente abajo era oh tan ruidosa.
Solamente pudiendo si su amor
Oh mi dios siento el amor

El amor a través de este mundo, oh mi
El amor dentro de este mundo wo-oh
Amo este mundo, ohhh sí
El amor entre este mundo

MEMORANDUM IN A CRUET

Le bébé, bébé, peut vous sentir l'amour à travers...
... à travers le monde que

certains disent que c'est un endroit horrible
Certains disent que c'est un endroit déloyal
Certains disent qu'elles détestent cet endroit
Tout que j'ai obtenu de dire est amour d'I cet endroit

Comme je voyage parmi ces terres
Je semble l'amour de tous que je peux
C'est tout à fait une vue à voir
Puisque l'amour rend me la sensation si libre

Comme mon endroit était au-dessus de ces nuages
Les personnes ci-dessous étaient l'OH si fort
Seulement pouvant si leur amour
Oh mon Dieu je sens l'amour

L'amour à travers ce monde, OH mon
L'amour dans ce monde OE-OH
J'aime ce monde, ohhh oui
L'amour parmi ce monde

Baby, Baby, kann Sie der Liebe über glauben...
... über der Welt, die

einige Leute sagen, daß dieses ein schrecklicher Platz ist
Einige Leute sagen, daß dieses ein gefährlicher Platz ist
Einige Leute sagen, daß sie diesen Platz hassen
Alle, die ich erhielt zu sagen, ist I Liebe dieser Platz

Wie ich unter diesen Ländern reise.
Ich scheine die Liebe von allen, die ich kann
Es ist durchaus ein Anblick, zum zu sehen
Weil die Liebe mich Gefühl so frei bildet

Wie mein Platz über diesen Wolken war
Die Leute folgend waren lautes OH- so
nur in der Lage seiend, ihre Liebe wenn
OH- mein Gott glaube ich der Liebe

Die Liebe über dieser Welt, mein OH-
Die Liebe innerhalb dieser Welt wo-OH-
Ich liebe diese Welt, ohhh ja
Die Liebe unter dieser Welt

MEMORANDUM IN A CRUET

Baby, Baby, kan du føler de elsker accross ...
... Over hele verden

noen folk si dette er en gruelige sted
Noen folk si dette er en farlige sted
Noen folk sier de hater dette sted
Alle jeg det si er jeg elsker dette sted

Som jeg reise blant disse akrer
Jeg synes den kjærlighet fra alle jeg kan
Det er ganske en øine å se
fordi den kjærlighet gjør meg føler så gratis

Som min plass var fremfor disse skyene. folket
nedenfor var oh så høyt
Bare å være i stand til å bør deres kjærlighet
Oh min Gud jeg føler de elsker

De Elsker over denne verden, oh min
Den Kjærlighet med i denne verden wo-oh
Jeg elsker denne verden, ohhh ja
Den kjærlighet blant denne verden

Last Night

I Hope Still You Know
That We Met A Year Ago
Awhile Since I Saw You Last
Let's Start From Our Past
I Gave You My Heart
Twice We Fell Apart
I Blame Myself For All
Tomorrow I'll Call

You're My Best Friend
Now In Love Again
I Give My Love To You
I'll Spend My Life With You
She Is The One
Who Is Always Fun
To This One Boy
You Still Bring Me Joy

Last Night, I Thought It Through
Please Bring Me Back To You
Last Night, I Thought It Through
I'll Bring My Love To You

Last Summer At The Show
I Hope This Year You Will Go
So What Can Happen Once Again
To Be With You, I'll Ditch My Friends
Second Time Was A Kiss
You Are Mine, I Will Miss
You Are Perfect In Every Way
So Now Let's Just Go And Lay, Again

Bring A Smile To Your Face
Take This At An Easy Pace
Fill You With Everything
Don't Stop Making My Heart Ring
Game I Will
Never Kill
What We Had
Losing Is Bad

Last Night, I Thought It Through
Please Bring Me Back To You
Last Night, I Thought It Through
I'll Bring My Love To You

We'll Last Forever
I'll Leave Never
In Love 'Til I Die
Losing You Had Me Cry
Maybe On This Night
We Will Shed Some Light
Again We Go At It
I Throw My Heart In It

MEMORANDUM IN A CRUET

Lose Myself In Your Eyes
I Won't Give You Any Lies
You've Been In My Thoughts
Since The Night We Fought
Keep Near To Me
On My Knees
Pleading To You
Can't Stop Loving You

Last Night, I Dreamt Of You
Us Together At 22
Last Night, I Got A Clue
You Wanted Me to Be With You

Last Night, It All Came Out
I Just Want To Go and Shout
Last Night, I Left It Out
My Love Came Out In That Shout

Last Night, It Came At Last
Together Again Like Our Past
Last Night, I Loved You So
Tomorrow I'll Love You More

Carnival

I'm tired of waiting in line
For the world to be mine

My life is on a wild roller coaster
Forever the suspense to reach the top
Displayed elsewhere on every poster
But so fast and quick the drop

Moments of excitement on this ride
Separated by challenges in disguise

Like a carnival, call all be gone in a night
Such as life, the house of mirrors and fright

In the middle, there is a wishing well
Hoping to escape my thoughts on this carousel
Around, Around, Here we go again
Tonight I found, here we go again

Getting dizzy and bound to puke
On an emotionless ride mono-hue fluke
Yet with amounts of saturation
To fulfill momentarily satisfaction

Roller Coaster, Drop Me Fast
Carousel, Forever Lasts
Ferris Wheel, Here we go again
Convenience Stands, Follow The Rows Again

Afternoon Vacations

I believe in taking afternoon vacations
To fill the void with an indescribable sensation

I believe in taking afternoon vacations
To fill the void with an indescribable sensation

Now I fall down on the street
Someone propped me back unto my feet
When I wiped the tears from my eyes
My high school took me by surprise

I believe in taking afternoon vacations
To fill the void with an indescribable sensation
I believe in taking afternoon vacations
To fill the void with an indescribable sensation

Living in a dream left from my own
Getting away to find my true home

As The Rain

Friends, I'm so sorry,
For what happened to what we had
For what we did, and what we loved

Where am I, in life right now
I finally realized what I got to do now
Move along, with my life
Time to show the world, what I'm like

Waking up, every single day
There has to be, a price to pay
With every night, I feel the hurt
From a strong yet, lonely heart

As, the rain swallows/surrounds me
I find it too hard to see
the sun's beams of light
I cannot withhold this fight
I'm drowning constantly
Someone please save me
Soul is drenched and weathered
I cannot move on any farther

Now friends, I'm so lonely, for what we need, again
What we had, what we did, and for what we have, ever-loved

Another challenge, every single day
There has got to, be a way
To make it through, and to the top
To make thy stress, completely stop

As, the rain swallows/surrounds me
I find it too hard to see
The sun's beams of light
I cannot withhold this fight
I'm drowning constantly
Someone please save me
Soul is drenched and weathered
I cannot move on any farther

The rain slows around me
Slightly easier to see
The sun's blinding light
I can start withholding this fight
Downing not so quickly
I do not need you to save me
Soul is dying and weathered
I can go on, a little farther

Suddenly the rains gets worse, around me
This time I cannot see
The sun, this time, there is no light
I think I lost the fight
Drowned, this time completely
It's too late to save me
Soul is drenched, weathered
My soul is drenched, and weathered
Woahhh.... I cannot see
Woahhh... I lost this fight
Woahhh... Too late to be saved
Woahhh... My soul is weathered

C ist für Cassie

Nachricht auf myspace
Sagte sie hat mich betrogen
Sie gefickt anderen Kerl
Denen war besser als ich

C ist für cassie
C is für Fotze
Cassie ist eine Holle
Von heisse Fotze

Hallo meine Liebe
Ich habe an dich gedacht.
Was sagst du?
Versuchen wir es noch einmal,
Ist das gut?
Ja, das ist gut.

Nur zwei Wochen in unserer Beziehung,
Nur zwei wochen und sie betrogen wieder.

C ist für cassie
C ist für Fotze
Cassie ist sehr sexy
Und eine heisse Mose.

Three Week Love

On day one, we went on a date
On day two, we stayed up real late
On day three, I rubbed your feet
On day four, you beat my meat
On day five, we're in the park
On day six, my names not mark
On day seven, this week is over
You're my special four leaf clover.

On day one, we laughed with fun
On day two, I'm kissing you
on day three, We're under a tree
On day four, you wanted more.
On day five, we're feeling alive
On day six, Gifts of Guitar Picks
On day seven, we're in Heaven
After These Weeks, I feel in love

On day one, Just the park again
On day two, Just my house again
On day three, never had a better kiss
On day four, if you left, I'd miss
On day five, feeling the end
On day six, we were still friends
On day seven, you gave me a shove
Oh Princessa, my Three Week Love

Nazi Jesus

Nazi Jesus, straight from Zombieland
Run for the hills, we're going to all be dead
Concentration Camps, Burn the fire!
Build a Wall, For Our Desires!

Nazi Jesus, Straight From Hell
Live with him in a burning' hell
Concentration Camps, Burn the fire!
Build a Wall, For Our Desires!

Nazi Jesus, Here To Save
Nazi Jesus, From the Grave
Nazi Jesus, Here To Save
Nazi Jesus, From the Grave

Adolf Von Amedica
Hitler Of America

Ember Chambers Strap Us Within
Let us out now who gave our sins
Morbid memories haunt us here
We're in a hell, trapped with fear
A light glows so far away
A Star perhaps, but who's to say?
We're chained here for now
Spending our days in bows

Nazi Jesus to conquer these lands
Imprison us all, souls be dead

Goddess

You're a very beautiful girl
Want you more than a pearl
You are much cooler than me
Someday maybe you will be

No one I rather be with but you
You're the only one cooler than me
Maybe someday you'll love me too
Might be awhile so we'll see

If there is another day like this
Just some other day I'd miss
Being with the most beautiful girl
In the whole-wide world

No one I rather be with but you
You're the only one cooler than me
Maybe someday you'll love me too
Might be awhile so we'll see

On the phone I talk to you
To let you know how much I love you
I'd do anything to be back with you
I always try and end up like a fool

No one I rather be with but you
You're the only one cooler than me
Maybe someday you'll love me too
Might be awhile so we'll see

There is only one girl for me and that's you
We will be back together hopefully
Maybe someday you'll come back to me
Until that day, did you ever love me?

Writer's Block

I wish I knew how to write a decent song
I haven't been able to write in so long
To grab a hold of the words so deep
Blocked In Again, to even speak

The truth is embedded in me, but I
do not know what it is, So I
sit down in comfort and begin, do I
have a clue of what to even say to you?

Blocked In My Head And Cannot Get Out
Better Off Dead Mhmmm... I Doubt
We Have To Find A Way To Speak So Loud
That Our Whispers Will Move The Clouds

Sitting alone with a notebook and even he
Doesn't have a friend that will die for me
My heart beats a verse that leaves home Earth

Friday Night

All alone on a Friday night
She has a feeling that just isn't right
He's making out with different girls
Running away from his own world

Every single day
He cheats on her
What is this?
I'm much better

I just found out what's been going on
He's with a different one at the brink of dawn
This just isn't right and I'm ready to fight
But I think I'll tell her first

She doesn't believe me
She just got pissed off
I keep on trying
She thinks I'm lying
Now what to do
I feel like a fool
I have to convince her
That I'm much better

Are You Out There?

Been searching for so long- *(So long)*
Staring at the sky- *(at the clouds, the birds, Above)*
Wondering if True Love is a lie
Looking up as the clouds above *(looking up, praying for love)*
Praying for a love sent to me, *(like a dove)*
Trying to believe in Destiny

Are you out there? Looking for me? Out there, searching too-
Are you out there? Praying for love that's true?

I've been waiting for the other half for me
been patient for the soul meant for me
Are you listening to me spirit- filled cry-
Thinking fate may be a lie?
Where, are you tonight? *(I'll treat you right)*
Where's our love tonight? *(I'll treat you right)*

Are you out there? Looking for me?
Out there, searching too-
Are you out there? Praying for me?
For a love- a love, so true-

Are you out there?
I'm here, *(I'll be there)*
I'm waiting, *(I'll be waiting)*
Just for you, *(I'll treat you, right-)*
Only for a love I know that's true.

Hey Dad

Hey dad,
I thought you had changed
But I guess I was wrong
When you walked right out
I started to pout
You said you'd never
Come back to us again
Why'd you have to run?
Away from me again

Our door is wide open only for you
Shunned me out of your life I came unglued
You might've said I'd show them
But what is there to show
Come on you have a wife
She deeply loves you

Alyssa

Alyssa Alyssa
You're so fine
Alyssa-
Always on my mind

Come on Alyssa,
Come be mine
It's unofficial,
but I think it's time

Alyssa! Alyssa!
Oh! Oh! Alyssa!
Oh, Alyssa!
You and Me
Oh, Alyssa!
You and Me-
Alyssa Alyssa
Its been too long
Alyssa-
Nothing can go wrong

I'm the boy for you
So why don't you-
Oh Alyssa
Take my hand, tonight?

Alyssa Lets make this
Official tonight
Alyssa Lets make this
Official tonight

Oh Alyssa
Wont you be
My Girlfriend
Officially

MEMORANDUM IN A CRUET

MEMORANDUM IN A CRUET

Act IV
The Lost Chapters

One Million Miles

I woke up today, a million miles away from where I was yesterday.

Wondering where I was, and how I got here. In a limbo, from my past to my future. This everyday vacation has gotten me farther than I have ever gotten before. This is what I call the Adventure.

And when it is safe... close your eyes... open your mind...
Letting this journey begin

Praise for Days

I sing a song that is full of praise
For you My God, For all of my days

I'm Giving This Song To You
Please Take me With You Somewhere
I'm Living This Song For You
Please Take Me With You Anywhere

I would like to thank Humanity
For the language, science, math and more
But history is the one thing not for sure

AiR

If I could choose, to live here or there
I would probably pick there
So I could go pretty much anywhere
Going to take myself everywhere
To wash my hair, new ones to care
Playing musicals at the fair
Come close to me, to you I dare
I might just pretend to care
With a hug, like a bear
Saddle me, on this chair
You smell like a pear
I have nothing to wear

Forgot My Check

I wish I may, I wish I might
Let Me Become a Man Tonight
Vacation At Grandma's, oh yes, oh boy!
Going to go see my best friends, oh joy!

School was not the same as before
I had expected it to be so much more
To live again became my threat
Losing to God's wrathful bet

My friends became my escape from this
My home life began to hate all of this
Living my life in Joy with friends
My family is going to be my end

I've seen the truth from the pawn slips
I showed you pain as I slit my wrists
The gun he held as tears rolled down his face
As he walked out that door with my only bass

With Aldan to cash my last slip
Then I realized I had forgotten my check
A nervous tweak, as I bit my lip
I called payroll to get on deck
My check was cashed, how is that so?
A man at 40 can be so low
This was just the start of this
I learned to hate because of this

I Got None

I got no job
I got no girl
My life is weak
To the world

I got no car, nor a phone
I got no help, nor love, oh please

I got no money
I cannot eat
I got no need
Just a heartbeat

Got a friend that gets me high
He won't ever leave me alone
Got a grandma but only
She cannot be left alone

Stuck to Help
Chained in a well
Trained to Help
Chained to a well

Move On

It Hurts, It Hurts, It Hurts, It Hurts,
It Hurts, It Hurts, It Hurts, It Hurts,
It Hurts, It Hurts, It Hurts, It Hurts,
It Hurts, It Hurts, It Hurts, To Say,
Goodbye

Been counting the, days I've been with,out you
1, 2, 3, 4
Been counting the, days that you've been, gone
1, 2, 3, 4
Been counting the, days I've been with,out you
1, 2, 3, 4
Been counting the, days since you left,- me
1, 2, 3, 4

It is time to, let you go
HERE I, GO
I need to move on, with- my-, life

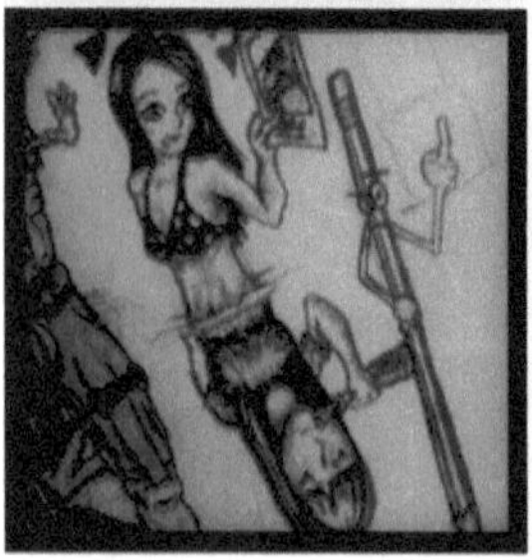

Now and Forever

There's no one as pretty as you
Since you left I've been feeling blue
So please listen to my plea
I hope you'll come back to me

Your red hair is so beautiful
You got the loveliest green eyes
I will always be faithful
None of these are lies

Your red is so beautiful
You got the loveliest green eyes
I will always be faithful
none of these are lies

Someday you might see
If you ever come back to me
I will always love & never leave you
My promise to you, that this true

Even though you are not mine
Could I kiss you one last time
Just before you go, Just to show
How much I Loved You.

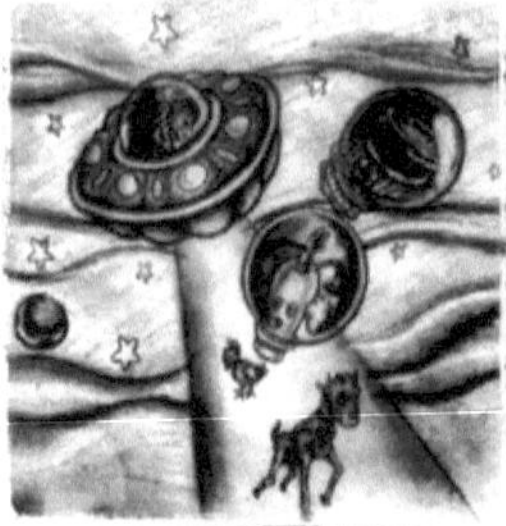

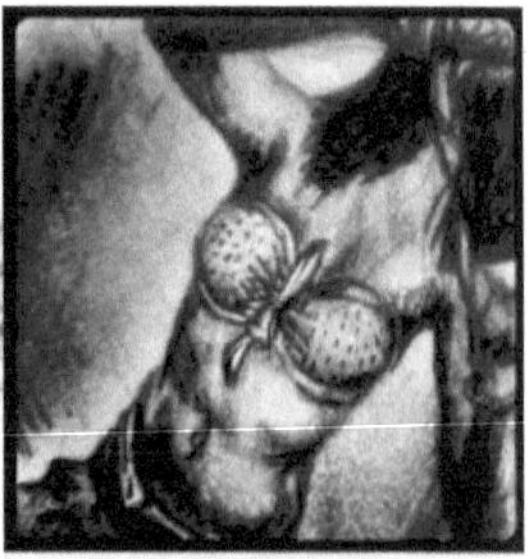

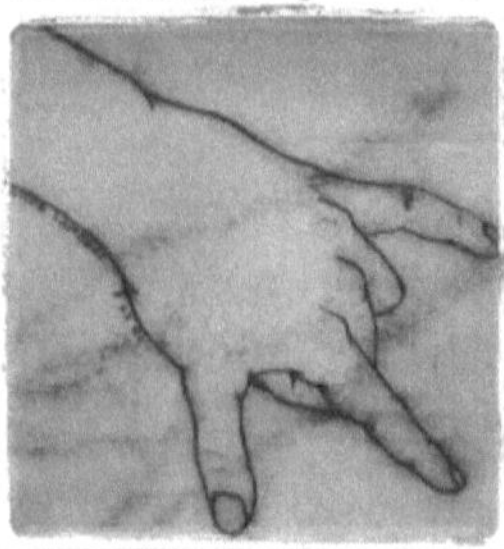

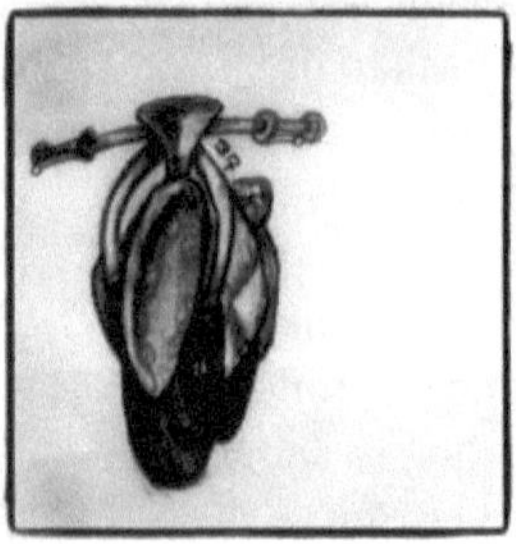

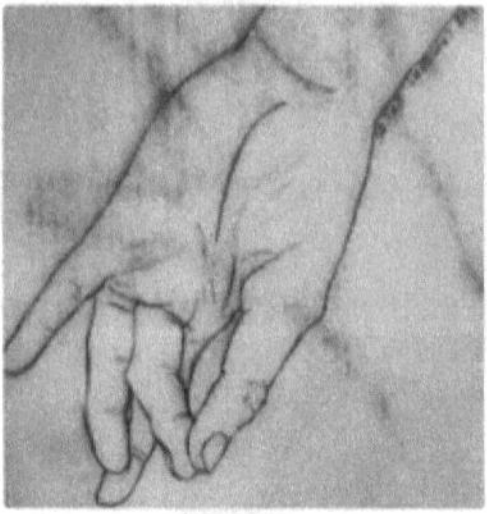

One Hundred Suns

A Relationship for One Hundred Suns
It seems as if it has just begun
A Relationship for One Hundred Suns
It seems like it has just begun

With One Hundred Suns, It has Just begun
A tale with my princess, in a world of dreams
With One Hundred Suns, It has Just begun
My wish came true, oh so it seems

The most beautiful thing, I have ever seen
Is you my dear
I'll write to you and sing, Like a machine
I need you here

The resting of the sun on the turn of my life
Blushing and smiling I just met my wife

One Hundred Suns have risen
One Hundred Sun have set
We'll meet again one day
I'm sure of this bet

Sixty moons have passed us by
I'm proven to you that I can fly
I'm the prince, I'm the Man
I'm the king of these lands

Ninety Suns Have Set and I'm going insane
Breaking your window and calling you names

On the drive home, I drove you home
With all my power I drove 21 hours
King of the Dorsey's, drove me home
Told him the truth of a candy sour

I hate you so much, I love you so
I understand that you have to go
I yelled at you so very loud
Only God knows if I'm proud

The night when I heard
you scream, I LOVE you so much
You, My Love, Its just a dream
But, I Love you as well

The most beautiful thing, I have ever seen
Is you my dear
I'll write to you and sing, Like a machine
I need you here

. With One Hundred Suns, It has Just begun
A tale with my princess, in a world of dreams
With One Hundred Suns, It has Just begun
My wish came true, oh so it seems
With One Hundred Moons, I Need You Here
The end is soon, so please don't fear

MEMORANDUM IN A CRUET

One Hundred suns have passed us by
One hundred moons have lit your face
One Hundred suns have already died
One hundred suns rising the bass

One hundred times the sun has set
Princess why must you say not yet?
One hundred times the sun has risen
Baby can this all be forgiven?

The night when I heard
you scream, I LOVE you so much
You, My Love, It's just a dream
But, I Love you as well

I hate you so much, I love you so
I understand that you have to go
I yelled at you so very loud
Only God knows if I'm proud

With One Hundred Suns, It has Just begun
A tale with my princess, in a world of dreams
With One Hundred Suns, It has Just begun
My wish came true, oh so it seems

The most beautiful thing, I have ever seen
Is you my dear
I'll write to you and sing, Like a machine
I need you here

One hundred times the sun has set
Princess why must you say not yet?
One hundred times the sun has risen
Baby can this all be forgiven?

Orange Traffic Cone

My cousin and I Adventure (that's right)
To find that pretty orange (tonight)

Block The Street
Lose The Heat
Block Da Street
Lose Da Heat

At a hectic pace to move these cones
on a mission, than we're home
Kings of this world and the cones
Got to move quick, cannot be found

Red and Blue, Blue and Red
Coming Quick, We're Dead
Red and Blue, Blue and Red
Coming Quick, We're Dead

Step By Step
We're Gonna Make It
Step by step
Mission Completed

Sandwich

Sandwiches are what I eat
My transportation, is by feet

Bologna, Cheese, Ham and more
Maybe a sandwich with an apple core
Cinnamon, peanut butter, hazelnut
I am what I eat, I'm a little nut

Peanut butter jelly and cheese
Oh no thanks, that's not for me

Small, Petite and Sweet

Small Petite, Really Really Sweet

My Lady Is Small
Cute, Petite
Really Really Sweet
She cannot be beat

The Lie

How different is the world going to be
As time passes for you and me

Remember when we would just set to cry
Upon the night when you found the lie
Remember when our love was so fierce
Whips and chains will break my back this year

Superstar

See the girl in the mini-skirt?
Well, she's a Superstar
See the Vuitton on her shirt?
Well, she's a Superstar

Hear her lungs enlighten a tune?
Well, she's a Superstar
Hear Her Name across the moon?
Well, she's a Superstar

Feel the way she likes to move
Well, she's a Superstar
Feel the way she makes the groove
Well, she's a Superstar

Smell her Paris Hilton perfume
Well, she's a Superstar
Smell the douche in her panty-loons
Well, she's a Superstar

Taste her kiss of love or death
Well, she's a Superstar
Taste her breathe hinted of a chef
Well, she's a Superstar

Sick and Tired

So I lay here in my bed alone
Everything connects, preparing me for what?
You're my Spirit, I walk for you Jesus

Where are you taking me?
I looked like my hero, is that a sin?
I'm tired of the people telling me who to be
I'm sick of the ones telling me what to do
Who pretend that I'm something I'm not

I'm sick of feeling down
I'm tired of feeling angry
I hate feeling alone
I love myself, way too much

Jesus, Take me by the hand,
I took the time to know myself
Please, Take me by the hand
Take me down the right path

Snow

It is Cold, oh yes I know
Keep me warm, take off my clothes
It is cold, shiver me timbers
Keep me warm by the fire

Let's Spend All Day, Playing in the Snow
Let's drive 'til dawn, before you have to go

Last Song

That is the last song, I 'm sorry for you
But I do have a great tale to tell to you
Of Triumph, Passion, and Despair
Learning to see how some don't care

Need a Job

Having My Artwork Pay for my bills
Mikey Thirty Seven has the will
Having My Music pay for my food
Mikey Thirty Seven makes the rules

Working from nine to five, A burden to stay alive
We all work so hard, Just to finally die

We need a job, to eat some food
We need a job, to sleep with shelter
We need a job, to have a good mood
We need a job, to avoid some whether

Lonely Nights, Where it seems like we're going no where
Day after day, Face after Face, its just all the same
I'm stuck in a rut that chains me down, maybe, forever
An ache in my head, a papercut, such, such, such a shame
Hand in hand, we will get through this
Man to Man, we will write a list
Hand in hand, we will arrive in peace
Man with Man, we will cover a lease

Check after Check, seems like I'm going to be there soon
Bill after bill, I barely make it through a month
Staring at the stars, asking why to a crimson moon
When will I make it through, will it be after lunch?

Hand in hand, we will get through this
Man to Man, we will take what's his
Hand in hand, we will live in peace
Man to Man, We won't share sheets
Man with Man, we be livin' in peace

U + I = Y

When I close my eyes, all I can see is your face.
It is by no surprise, that I'm still in love is the case.
When I close my eyes, you're waltzing across my path.
Baby, I have no lies, I'd do it all for you, check the math.

You plus I, equals true love.
I'm your guy, sent from above.
You minus I, equals true hate.
You're my gal, it's our fate.

When I close my eyes, all can I see is your face,
Accelerating the beat of my heart at a Mach pace.
When I close my eyes, you're there in my dreams.
I miss you too much, all I can do is yelp and scream.

You times I, equals heaven on Earth.
We can fly, like darts made by nerf.
You divided by I, leaves prime remainders.
We're not prime, with such remainders.

E equals M C squared, leaves me rapping,
As if you once cared, leaves me rapping.
If I'm the X and you're the Y.
The equation concludes I'm an exponential guy

Lilly and Caesar

Once upon a time a girl named Lilly fell into a pond.
Once upon a time a boy named Caesar lived with his mom.
They loved to cry as they laughed so hard,
They stole Enrique's credit card.
They stole some shoes and a fish, they had a secret wish.
On 11:11 Lilly and Caesar , and to you who sees. I wish you all the best, let's lose the fleas.
A fairytale to them but does it seem real, when will you have your next meal?
Any similarities between a Lilly and a Caesar, are completely coincidental. Because these two are ever so gentle.
They ride their ponies with sparkling green manes. This horse is part of what gave them fame.
For you see, it wasn't anything about themselves, for what they grabbed gave them wealth.
They stole some shoes and a fish, they had a secret wish.
One lives alone at the sea. The other one wishes to be me. They'd cast their dreams aside, sneaking away to go and hide.
As the legend was told, they weren't very much. Rumors like high school and such. They became like a monk, and one like a nun.
Lilly became aware of such pride. She drank whisky as she'd hide.
Caesar became drunk with the Love, he became a curse from what's above.
Lilly changed her name, again and again. Caesar stumbled face firs t in acidic sin. Seven years gone, he feels alone. She feels so alone.
Caesar rode a go-kart down the Great Wall of China. Lilly now strip s in little china. They hear the laughs of kids, and their screams.
They try to change the world like Romeo and Juliet. They'll take what's stinky and wet. A goal to the moon, to them feels soon. Take off is at noon.
At the terminal they accidentally meet. Their jaws drop to their feet.

Ten minutes pass and Lilly begins to cry, Caesar just stood and then said hi.
They had empires on the each side of this planet, nicknamed each after Janet. They had feuds, all of the time. They said goodbye to what ...
They sat down in the cockpits. Caesar had stinky armpits. Lilly's fish felt so raw, but they were locked-jaw.
For this did not matter to them, it just pretty much does not matter to them. They do not care for you nor I, they will kill you at good bye.
Lillie had harsh words to the world, when things got tough she would

rl.
But now here they are holding hands, and listening to his old band. The time for him has come at last, for he is passing gas.
The cockpit stunk but they flew this spaceship, all the way as he they did the whip.
They approach the moon and put on their space helmets, but first they eat their vomit. The nutrients, they said, were so good.
As they jump ship, to float to the moon. They do it in the nude.
For the death of Love, in such a place. Is everything but a waist.
Now at night, if you look close. You might just see a ghost. On the moon that is so far, but their souls have a 24 hour bar.

Deeper

Maybe I need to go deeper, to save your lives.
Blend with me an epic story, that shall never die.
Hear a legend of the Illuminati, the richest ones of our body.
Informing you of Agenda 21, it's to be the end of everyone.
Since H. W. Bush, this plan has stayed persistent.
Being passed by the following presidents.
We'll lose our rights, it's time to fight.
The Rockefellers know what I'm talking about, they funded woman's rights, no doubt.
Escalading the ones to tax, rich get richer to the max.
Dare to pick up the mic to preach,
Ascend into the 'Time to Teach'.
Make it smart, Clever as well, Make people believe you are hell.
Follow me, I'll give you some more.
Abandon now, breaking down your door.
Shouts that are just for fun, Screaming at the top of the lungs.

Gazing into your turntable eyes, morphing me while being hypnotized.
A Nirvana dream enchanting the young. Noosing my heart as it's hung.
Losing my soul during Armageddon, a luscious being, unhidden.
Saints loathing compromise. Hades is in disguise.
Craving for my desires to spoon, as we stare upon bricked heavens.
One day we'll breathe on the moon, avoiding our symphonic raven.

Meteors strike nukes on tainted trails, worldly passion ignites hail. Devastation brewing beneath the core, tribes in arms breeding encore.
Moments are constant in our minds, believing what we can find. A renaissance man that keeps true, but question is who are you?
Raise our thoughts to new heighths, for a utopia I shall fight.
Expression is key to spirituality, excel daily to be free.

It seems as if I should've been born 1000 years ago, this is the 1000th day that has told me so. Reincarnation exists, to finish thy list.
The mark of the beast will lie everywhere, Everyone on facebook stare. Facebook's cross is over there, Facebook has conquered everywhere.
I'm sorry that my ego come at you like so, Amazing how I can let it grow. One swift move, my haters are dead, now it is time to move ahead.
You're ridiculous, don't touch me there, it's not in that way, I care.
I'll give you a hug on this day, then we shall be on our way.
The Facebook suit is to complete their project, as to when we live thou's gadget. Finally thank God that we're here, Jesus's return is near.
Will you send me a letter to occupy, with some sarcasm, but no lies. Just drop with a 'hey', we'll talk about whatever you say.
It would be nice if we could just sit and talk, and perhaps take a relaxing walk. Sip some cocoa by a cozy fire, Aura of us, glistens high.

She Doesn't Sleep

On this day she's lost her will, breathing pain through subconscious gills.
Caught in between two directions, where is our reflection?

Sleepless nights as to where she waits for him, all she does is seem to worry within.
Alone all day in a solitude of hell, Developing mental math, Adding unwell.

If she did not have me there, she would be forever scared.
I hope she knows there, of how much I care.

She misses nights of sleep just to catch those moments with me, she rather have misery in company than let me free.

A mischievous mind that desires to serve, believing it's get purpose in this world.

I beckon no, I can handle this on my own, and through eleven dimensions I've grown.

I am not your dad, I am not your husband. But I'll be there to take your hand.

I need to live, I need to breathe, this world I must see.
I'm all that she has left, this is a sure bet.
I Love you so, don't you know?

Narrowing Down

Narrowing down an armada of songs,
that I've been working on for so long.
About time for the iTunes promotion,
the moment I set sail in the ocean.

I'm flabbergasted by the nuisance of work,
Should I be ashamed of the speech of a jerk.
Web design, illustrations, tunes, and service.
A renaissance man must remain impervious.

Paintings, drawings, photography.
A clothing line done by just me.
This poetry goes out to the thousands I've met.
I'm hitch hiking the trail of Haley's Comet.

Game

For my dear brothers, there's a way to get there, this we all know.
Together we'll put on the most epic show.
What was it that inspired me so hard, that lets me wield a strong bold heart. Tales told to the lands a far. There exists a man from Mars.

Operation unleashed devouring engagement. Conscious deities design arrangement. Nimbus passion consumes companions. Unbegotten crucified contention.

Where is the nerve that poses cringe, how may I knock your door off of it's hinge. Words deceive the legitimacy, I've befriended epiphany.

Our generation out numbers that of the baby boomers, the youth will inherit the earth is the rumor.
This game though is not for me, but it is what brought you to me, if you would take one moment to believe, you'll learn the ways to be free.

Let your hate aspire the clouds, let this piece of art die loud.
Adorn the change, in full range. People are feeding into my game.

The deities of the ten dimensions, today would live in detention.
We love you all, did I mention? We'll help guide to redemption.

Capitalistic rituals breed hate for desire, no matter what is said, it's a liar. Intangible being swaddling lust, rouge mission now a must.

To change the world into a new imperfection, forever and always in reflection. Image a ranch full of pigeons, debating over false religions.

This same man taught me to grow, and since you all talk, it just shows. Six of us who invite you all, even the ones who want us to fall.

An ego that twisted your mind, I'm sorry I hurt your kind. A man once said, please head to bed. Pretty soon you will be dead.

From her to her, her to him, and him to them. I found the room stacked full of gems. Ingenious and infamous we are, we're accidental stars.

If everything happens for a reason, how did I get to right here. A vacant parking lot, with echos to hear.

Go insane and you'll find what you need, let everyone watch you bleed. Straight from the book you read, I'll do my best with this lead.

Some want lightning, some enjoy fighting. I personally just love writing. Love and hate, real and fake, what does it really take?

Ten dozen places with one hundred faces, Lost track of all the places. Legion reborn from indonesia. Apologies for the amnesia.

Playing thus role, for all of you. Leaving the eye here with you. This next half is just for you. I shall open your mind too.

Open the floodgates at the brink of dawn. In an instant, mowed the entire lawn. Ambush the campsite with swift, another mountain to lift.

MEMORANDUM IN A CRUET

I would like to journey through a lush pasteur, where the streams flow peacefully, to see this entire continent in the midst of it's beauty. Journey across this entire country on bike. To learn as much as I may before my dying day, reach enlightenment, journey across this entire planet, ride a go kart down the great wall of china, race on the autobahn, become president, walking the path less chosen, a life filled with a million on the bucket list, leave a legacy, remove the closed minds which would make me closed minded :o a place that is peaceful filed, design create obsorb enhance teach, gather us all as one, experiences across the board, to search for a truth I may never receive. To look for my soul mate that may not exist. To support good causes. To raise everyone up into a utopia status, even if It makes me a martyr. to speak to an enormous crowd with gifts that'll change history.

Truth. Knowledge. Love.

If I was your man, you'd be treated like a princess everyday. I would bring you flowers, keep you cozy and warm. I'd hold the door for you and keep chivalry alive. I'd be there for you whenever you needed me, and keep you the happiest woman alive. My true colors, would be to live for you. Cherish our moments, and I promise that we'd make it through anything together. I used to write, by putting up a front. To avoid being hurt again. But the truth is, All woman are beautiful. I'll forever be the type to put you ahead of myself.

It's one of those nights where, if I don't act submissive there will be a fight. Can't I have a night to talk about this with a parental figure because my migraines are hitting hard. Which with the poor flow in some on those veins, I could have a stroke or heart attack. Both being highly hereditary. After everything I mentioned, why in God's name would I jump when you call. In Albert Einstein's words, I would be insane to come to you with trust again. Kind of like an abused puppy. I wish you no harm, because I do forgive you and I do love you. Our lives have to be completely separate though. I'm done with it.

www.ingramcontent.com/pod-product-compliance
Lightning Source LLC
Chambersburg PA
CBHW031419290426
44110CB00011B/444
9780692758854